ALEKSANDAR MILANOV

HOLISTIC SOCIETY

Sofia
Bulgaria
2017

Author: © Aleksandar Slavkov Milanov, 2017
www.newagecitizens.org
e-mail: alexander.milanov.nac@gmail.com
ISBN 978-619-90834-2-0

ALEKSANDAR MILANOV

HOLISTIC SOCIETY

This book is dedicated to all people who are going to blaze a trail for the emerging of the holistic society.

C o n t e n t

INTRODUCTION

We are witnessing unprecedented global challenges of above national character, which can't be fully resolved by using the modern paradigm of national egoism and corporate domination.

Examples of such challenges are the global warming; labor exploitation of most of the population; economic poverty of billions of people and the crescent conflict attitudes among different nations. There is a common feature to all of these problems and it is that they are a result of the functioning of the present socio-political system. There is an institutional infirmity and lack of motivation of the leading states and many of the large private corporations to face those global issues and this is the reason for not applying long-term solutions.

Now, more than ever, there is a need to rethink the principles and attitudes which are catalyzing these challenges and creating obstacles for a harmonious life for all.

Today we are seeing that the world leadership is neglecting the harsh consequences of its own actions and people are not given the opportunity to choose a higher path of development. It has become almost impossible for a human-being to avoid triggering a chain of human rights violation and pollution in all actions, even if the person is good-hearted and genuinely caring for people and nature. Behind every product that we are creating and consuming there is a colossal and traceable violation of rights. The desire of a political and economic control of a few had led to inability of formulating clear aims in front of all nations. A thorough definition of the public interest does not exist until today.

At the same time, parallel with these processes, we are witnessing an unprecedented access to information and knowledge. The personal development of separate individuals in order to find a balance in their relationships with others and with nature has become a prerequisite to rethink the social roles of human-beings in society. This positive personal transformation requires a global replacement of the present model of political governance and provides the opportunity of emerging of new social structures which are capable to relate to the world without exploiting it.

On the basis of this change lies the expansion of consciousness, the ability to feel what is humankind and how to develop harmonious relationships with other beings, including with the Earth. This view is capable of multiplication and implementation in every social structure and in all relationships without regards whether they are political, economic, cultural, religious, personal, or others.

All significant social revolutions were preceded by a major cultural shift in society which provides a different answer to the questions: "Who am I?" and "What is my role in society?"

Before describing the model of service to the whole and before introducing the principles of building of the holistic society, we should give a proper answer to the question: "Which are the driving forces in our society?"

CHAPTER 1

DRIVING FORCES IN SOCIETY

The driving force is the main reason to do or not to do something. It is the highest purpose around which we live in a certain way and which indicates what our system of values is. It lies behind our motivation to have a specific job, to communicate and to be with particular people, to educate ourselves, to choose entertainments and so on. It sets our attitude towards life, towards people, towards ourselves, towards God... towards everything. The driving force is our main source of energy and it predetermines our path of life, if we are following it. Therefore, if we know what our driving force is as individuals and as a society, we will be able to see the main direction in our life and to know what lies in front of us.

For a civilization the driving force shapes the stimulus which the ruling classes encourage among the ruled. It is present in all relationships and it is the cornerstone around which every civilization builds itself. The better we know it, the clearer we will be able to outline the positive and negative consequences that result from it.

The driving force predetermines the path of development of the society. Very often people are not fully aware of their motivation for certain behavior, but a simple observation and an honest evaluation of their actions will reveal it easily.

Absorbed by a variety of problems, many people are unable to see the directions of different social groups and society in general. If there is not in unison between the ethics of an individual and of society an existential dilemma arises for a person: to redirect a particular collective, or to detach from it, in order to preserve individual integrity.

Beside the period of emerging and developing of a certain community or a whole civilization, the driving force predetermines also the periods of decay, which signifies the necessity of transformation and internal reorganization of the community.

We can bring out two general and diametrically opposing driving forces which are present in the life of every person and every society. The first is the service to self and the second - service to whole.

Service to the Self

The building of a society which is developing (or degrading), led by the service to self as its main driving force is a conscious, purposeful and traceable process which forms the main social relationships in the past millenniums until present day.

This driving force is present into politics, international relations, economics, healthcare systems, education, jurisdiction, religion and so on. Every religious, political, economic or other form of social organization which instills fear for survival and encourages particular behavior with material rewards or provision of status, while regulating unwanted behavior with sanctions is a type of system in service to self - egoistic system. This conclusion is evident because it is relied on encouraging or restraining certain behavior of an individual or a group of people by influencing their ego and not by using measures for supporting the process of becoming aware of the consequences from their actions for the whole environment. One of the easiest ways to determine whether a social system is in the service to self is to look at the principles of distribution of the goods between its members. If they are allocated as a form of reward and deprived as a form of sanction, we can conclude that this is an egoistic system, because the management affects the ego of a person or an organization.

All presently enforced legal systems, most of the major religions and all capitalistic economy are functioning in the service to self. The domination of this driving force in our world is so total, that a person can be easily deceived that other motivation, other principle are unsustainable and different order will be impossible to last.

The most propagandized untruth in these systems is that egoism and self-interest are the deepest motivators for development and this attitude is maintained for thousands of years.

Significant part of the people who have preserved their humane attitudes and who are still capable to love, are reluctantly participating in an egoistic system mainly for two reasons: The first is because there is not an alternative proposal of a system in service to the whole and the second is that the goods that they are receiving for their work can be used for supporting close relatives and for the material secure of desired projects. Therefore, for this large group of people this participation is a compromise in which there is major ideological conflict, and not a choice, based of common principles for development.

The acceptance of this delusion that egoism is the strongest motivator for an absolute and irrefutable thesis premised limited set of instruments for leading the society. Their main characteristic is that they are influencing the ego of its members which leads to obscurity of the aims of the community. This leads to gradual social self-destruction, confining of the worldview and mutual alienation between the members of the society. These methods and instruments for influence are examined separately in the following chapters. Typical features are that often they are primitive, rude, illogical, restrictive to the freedom of the individual, even when his actions are directed towards positive changes in the society and will lead to harmonious creative expressions. The end wall of the prison in which the self-serving societies are becoming is the lack of feeling for purpose to live and not understanding the reason behind every form of social organizing. The egoistic social systems are placing survival as an end itself and as main purpose for participation in social relationships. This exact characteristic is present in all self-serving societies and it is the basis of transforming their members to become indifferent towards others, inhumane and competitive.

The irony of the rhythm of functioning of every self-serving system is that its values and actions which are meant to protect it at all costs are leading to its self-annihilation. The reason is that the subjects in the system who are achieving dominant position are realizing at certain point that they have become prisoners too and they are turning against it and all the subjects in it. If the rulers realize that their true purpose is to transform the system to a one that is in service to the whole, or to free its members to be included in such system, a lot of suffering can be prevented.

Despite the fact that survival is pointed as a main objective for all participants in these systems, it should be also at expense of others and the surrounding environment.

The system is presented to people only as a protector of society which can be true, if the relationships are constructed to serve the interest of the whole. When this is not done, it becomes the catalyst for the biggest conflicts and the cause of uncertainty and insecurity for the people. The declared ideals for humanism, higher ethics and equality have become empty slogans. The methods for governing inside an egoistic system include violation of rights of one ideal in order to protect another. An example is the violation of human rights of one group of people with the aim to increase the security of another.

The state is system of service to self which requires from its citizens to be obedient to its organs. Every participant has different value to the system and he is used for its stable existence. The legal order of the state functions as outside will imposed to the citizens which should be followed by them. Failure to fulfill it leads to repressive sanctions, which are always aimed at the rights of the disturber and almost always does not lead to change of his behavior patterns. The worldview which is maintained for the person about himself is that he is insignificant particle of dust in the system which gathers more value, if he makes others dependent from him. In economic relationships we see this principle among the private corporations which have to create dependence of the consumers to their products. The employees of the corporations who are realizing that in the present moment their needed by the organization are negotiating for a better remuneration, using the circumstance that their labor is needed.

Political leaders are acquiring social weight not because they have reasonable solutions for specific social issues and a vision for development, but because they are able to gather electorate, without regards what is their political message.

The principle of being valued because you are making others dependent by yourself is truthful also in promoting of religions. A religion is becoming socially acceptable and traditional, depending on the number of its followers, without regards how its doctrine is affecting them.

In order the governing methods which are influencing the ego of a person to be effective, it is necessary that he is raised to identify himself only by its ego. This will predetermine the direction for his search for happiness and how to find meaning of his life by focusing predominantly on the economic wealth and abilities to gain status in society.

The ability of a person to find a higher purpose in the affirmation of intransitive humanistic and ecological values is seen as weakness and naivety in the egoistic system, because he will not take full advantage to exploit certain situation.

The true reason for stimulating this driving force is, because when it becomes leading for the participants in the system, they are losing their sense of higher purpose and meaning of life and become maneuverable as pawns on a checkerboard. Their abilities to make a positive change in society are progressively reduced.

The more a person or an organization adopts the self-service as a leading driving force, the more they are detaching themselves from their humanity and higher purpose of existence.

In the end the person or the organization, accepting the ethics of the egoistic system forget or neglect the natural, decent attitude towards other beings, including the planet.

Every individual and every collective that do not have the sense of unity with all others, despite their differences, and who are living just for their survival, are used for someone's selfish interests.

Therefore, the suggestion that the most important direction for development is the selfish one is a subtle form of control over all participants in the system. This control is not necessary to be applied through the legal authority of a particular institution, but consists of maintaining attitudes and social model in which different communities are not able to find a common ground for cooperative co-existence.

When the participants in any social system are convinced that they should be guided by their self-interest and be prepared to disregard the interests of others, their behavior is always becoming harmful for the whole environment.

The ego, understood as a form which protects individual identity from the outer world, is not problematic as itself. Its balanced development is an absolute necessity for every individual and every organization in order to think themselves as separate, autonomous and protected reality. The biggest issue, which breeds the driving force of service to self, is placing the ego in the center of the person's existence, because this leads to assimilation of the environment to the one's ego. The result is reaching an extremely selfish attitude which blinds the person about the problems that he is creating and about the optimal solutions for them. Even if the interests of others are understood, they are neglected or used for taking advantage from the respective subject.

The stimulation of this driving force among all participants in egoistic system leads to injection of the environment and turning it in a zone for rivalry and conflict.

When the interest of a confined organization - family, corporation, party, religious or other, is pursued in way which are not in compliance with the interest of the whole, this is also a form of self-service. Some of these organizations are capable of building constructive and harmonious internal relationships between its members, but if they do interact selfishly with the outer world and trying to use it and victimize it, they are still operating as subjects in service to self. Therefore, if a person is devoted to his organization and is working selflessly for its development, but it is functioning in the service to self, his participation is still sustaining the same driving force. It is not enough a person to be unselfish to avoid being part of the egoistic driving force, but it is needed the overall effect of the organization he is working in to achieve beneficial influence to the environment through developing of the whole.

The driving force of service to self is leading to twisted identification of the social priorities. When it is guiding an organization the result is protecting ill functioning status quo at the expense of the whole environment which is gradually harmed more and more. A typical example of this behavior in global scale is the lack of will on behalf of the states in the fight against climate change and the absence of an overall plan for transforming the economy, so that it becomes socially fair and environmentally friendly.

The egoistic systems consider the animals, the plants and Earth as things which can be used by humans here and now. Insignificant are the legislative changes in few states for shifting this vision towards them. It remains predominant the understanding that they are primarily an economic resource, which can be used for creating dependence of large groups of people, because of their need of food.

The unity in a system of service to self is achieved when people accept that they will be used for selfish purposes, but are granted the right to use others as well. Management in such systems is the planning of exploitation. It includes analysis for what purposes and to what extent someone can be used for selfish reasons.

The development of the participant is directed and restricted, according to the needs of the system. This means that if the system needs large amount of low-qualified workers, it has to make sure that people are dropping out from the education system and are coerced economically to look for the corresponding position as a worker. Modern Western societies are ghettoizing large groups of their minorities and are encouraging illegal immigration in order to constrain them to occupy the low-level positions of the labor market.

Another remarkable flaw in egoistic systems is that many problems are necessary for justification of its organs and therefore solving them fully is an unwanted result. Examples of such social problems are examined in the following chapters.

Service to the Whole

If service to self, namely egoism, is well known characteristic of the individual and programmed way of thinking in governing the social processes, the service to the Whole requires more thorough description. The known approaches and methods for managing a state or a private business unjustifiably ignore this guiding force. In the next chapters it will be presented what would be the positive developments for society in general, if the driving force service to the Whole is integrated into different social structures.

Can we define rationally what the Whole is? Who is the subject, whose interest we protect as supreme and with priority over all others? What is placed as a core ideal in the center of the social system? How are we supposed to organize a society in order to be called holistic (in service to the Whole)? Do we have examples of social models which are developed by this driving force?

Let us define the Whole through its parts, which means through understanding who the subjects in it are. These are all living beings that the members of the corresponding system are aware of and for whom it is reasonable to assume that will emerge. It consists of all human-beings, animals, plants and other creatures that we are finding. The Whole comprises also the Cosmos, all universes, galaxies, planets, Earth. Among its subjects are the living beings from the past, those in the present and those that might be in the future. The concept of a living being usually is associated with a biological creature. If it is scientifically proven that do exist other conscious beings that do not have the known biological structure from Earth, they should also be considered as part of the Whole and subjects of the holistic model. More details about the subjects of the holistic model are presented in chapter two.

In order to provide proper answers to the questions above, it is necessary first of all to clarify what motivation stands in the core of the driving force service to the whole and what attitude it creates for the individual and for the society.

At the deepest level and in the center of this driving force stands the knowledge about the unity of all, the existence of a common Source of life and the ability of the individual to perceive itself as its unique manifestation. This knowledge and intuitive feeling forms an aspiration for building harmonious relationships among the participants which will support the optimal development of all.

This unity does not deprive from individuality the subjects, neither standardizes them, but recognizes their equal importance and encourages their creative and unique development in a direction which is respectful for others. It should be distinguished from the imperative unification, typical for the egoistic systems, which deforms the participants and turns them into survival individuals who are exploiting the environment.

Therefore, the identity, that forms the driving force service to the whole, is beyond selfish pursuing of egoistic objectives, but extends into the understanding of belonging to the whole environment.

The service to the whole should also be distinguished from the impersonal view and heartless relationship towards people. The difference with the motivation of service to self is that the person does not achieve prosperity for himself and his loved ones on the expense of others.

It is impossible and more importantly unnecessary for a person to try to resolve all problems in the world. The service to the whole does not mean to overload yourself with huge problems and responsibilities, neither is related with taking the burden of someone else. It is timely local action in the present environment which leads to global harmonization of the whole system.

The correct name of this driving force is "in service to the whole" and not "in service to others", because the last excludes the person from the scope. This exclusion is wrong and undesirable, because he himself bares the highest responsibility of his own development and only he has the freedom to choose its direction.

On the basis of the knowledge of the unity of all, the individual develops his attitude not only to consider and respect the interests of others, but also adequately and altruistically to satisfy them through the exercising the relationships that they do have. This type of interaction between the individuals leads to their harmonious development and positive change of the whole environment.

One of the main distinctions between both driving forces is that the service to the whole requires balancing one's personal interest with those of the others and satisfying it by finding mutually beneficial solutions, while the service to self is related with taking advantage from the interests of others in order to gain for yourself.

The egoistic structures rely on institutionalized authority to form the reality and attitudes in society, instead of providing proper instruments for the people to do that by themselves. In order to achieve this level of obedience among its members, the egoistic structure propagandizes absolute trust in the established sources of information, because they are controlled.

The social structure which is functioning in the service to the whole on the other hand relies on providing the necessary instruments to the participants for building wide, rich and critical worldview. The persons who have developed an expertise in certain area are encouraged to provide their in-depth knowledge and point of view, but at the same time all others are free to choose how to evaluate the conclusions of those experts. The critical thinking is required in the systems of service to the whole and neglected in the systems of the service to self. This important difference between both forms of community organizing draws the conclusion that the egoistic system is dogmatic and imposing whereas the holistic is creative and respective.

While the egoistic system values the amount of energy a person is able to take from the others, most often in the form of money, the holistic system values the quality and quantity of energy a person is providing for the whole.

On a personal level, one of the most certain ways to understand what driving force is guiding us in the choice of a specific profession is, if we can answer in the affirmative of the following questions:

1. Do I contribute sufficiently well for the benefit of the society by conducting my work activity?

2. Was I going to practice the same profession, if I was financially secured and there was no economic coercion whatsoever?

3. Am I going to practice the same profession even if I receive a very generous offer which would provide me with more money, but the new job would benefit the interests of the society much less?

The driving force of service to the whole is transferring the individual to new levels of self-awareness and self-realization. This is a result from cultivating the sense of unity between him and the environment which can be perceived as expansion of consciousness.

Until today there is not historical evidence which can show that a state is governed by stimulation of the driving force of the service to the whole. Despite that fact, we can find one particular social structure which functions very successfully by implementing this force of inspiration. It is the loving family.

There are many types of families in which are build harmonious relationships between their members. In the family that serves as a good example for a social structure exists love, mutual respect, recognition of the interests of its members, trust and good communication. In short, this family is referred as loving. This form of social organization is known to many people. For it is typical that is avoided the rivalry between the members and it is substituted with cooperation and finding the proper family role for every member. The relationships in it are firm and are characterized with a high level of trust. The motivation for developing the relationships and improving them is high among all participants. The loving family manages to function well when selfish attitudes of its members are not leading and such actions are avoided. The satisfaction and joy from the unselfish service which benefits the whole family and all its members are giving us the grounds to consider this social structure as an example of community which builds its internal relations in service to the whole.

The qualities which every participant is developing in the loving family include honesty, respect, care for others, kindness and others. Therefore, it is visible that the proper functioning of this social system builds a positive character among its members in a way that their spiritual potentials are revealed. It is possible to use partial aspects of this social model as an example of structuring bigger communities, including private corporations and even states.

It is absolutely possible a family to be kind and caring only about its own members and unscrupulous towards outside people. For example, a dictatorial family or exploitive family corporation may have an internal atmosphere of understanding and support, but inhumane terror to be predominant against their subordinates and the outside world. Consequently, besides internal relations, external too should be caring the positive characteristics, mentioned above, so that a community to be regarded as one of service to the whole.

Huge problem of the way larger communities are functioning until present day is that there are not well-designed global social models and macro-social system which are led by the driving force of the service to the whole.

The significance of the attitude towards God for building a social system

The choice what driving force will be leading for a society, respectively what social models and legal order will be implemented, is defined in very large extend by the attitude that a person has towards God and the outer world.

Max Weber, considered as one of the founders of the modern sociology, throws a light on the interrelationship between the attitude towards God and the basic principles of structuring the socio-economic system. He substantiates that the attitude of the majority of the participants towards God is determining to high extent the principles around which all social systems are constituted, including the economics.[1]

The attitude towards the divine creation and the understanding of the relationship between the man and the higher creative force are standing at the deepest level in the psyche and are fundamental for determining the political, social and economic systems of all societies. It is because the attitude towards the purpose of the institutional power and order is mirrored from the one towards God. The concept about the reason for divine creation is implemented in the design of all social models, respectively of all social systems.

---

1 Max Weber, *The Protestant Ethic and the Spirit of Capitalism*, Routledge Classics, 2001

For example in sociology and in other fields of social sciences it is examined the interrelationship between the industrial revolution, the free market initiative and the emerging of the Protestantism with all of its branches.

The direction of transformation (not formation) of capitalism in Western societies, embracing the values of entrepreneurship, rationalism, individuality, are rooted in large extent in the changed notion of the bond between God and the man and the role of church in the community.

Precisely the change of the attitude towards God and in particular the shift in understanding the bond between man and God lead to cardinally new direction of economic development, which benefits protestant communities at the account of native Americans and brought colored population.

The installment of atheism in scientific circles is much more a protest against dogmatic religious institutions and their pernicious involvement is science, than the realized understanding that something does not exist. There is not a serious scientist who is going to affirm that something does not exist, but he/she may provide arguments that what is presented as existing is not logically grounded. It would be fair to perceive scientific atheism as a reaction to the destructive influence of dominant religious institutions over humanity, but we should not be deluded that it is the actual attitude of the leading scientists. In fact the pioneers in science and great discoverers of the laws of Nature do have clearly defined understanding of God and their scientific endeavor is related to find a rational explanation of the divine creation. Typical representatives of the scientific community, who have their clear comprehension of science as a rational means of exploring God, are Isaac Newton, Immanuel Kant, Albert Einstein, Nikola Tesla and many others. In contradiction to their insights and published evidences of divine presence, many other representatives of scientific communities are willing to promote that whole science is atheistic and therefore the manifest world is accidental and everything is a random concurrence, instead of creative design.

Proof of the attitude that divine power exists and the universe is its creation of these notable scientists we can find in their own words and publications.

Isaac Newton, for example, is famous with his scientific discoveries in Physics, but he also had written religious treatises in which he shares his view of God:

„He, who thinks half-heartedly will not believe in God; but he who really thinks has to believe in God...The Supreme God is a Being eternal, infinite, absolutely perfect." [2]

The impulse which makes Einstein a brilliant scientist, who is absolutely convinced in the divine origin of the world, appears in his words too:

„I want to know how God created this world. I am not interested in this or that phenomenon, in the spectrum of this or that element. I want to know his thoughts. The rest are details." [3]

Nicola Tesla perceives the forces of mind as a concrete gift from God:

"The gift of mental power comes from God, Divine Being, and if we concentrate our minds on that truth, we become in tune with this great power. " [4]

Immanuel Kant have published a whole treatise which considers the existence of God as result of logical following and not just a blind faith: *"The One Possible Basis for a Demonstration of the Existence of God"(1763)*

From these quotes it is visible that the clear, meaningful, logic and balance concept of God, correspondingly of the world as divine creation, had shaped the minds of the most progressive scientists and thinkers of human civilization.

Despite this understanding in the religious and in the legal systems continue to be present the reflection of a dogmatic and oppressive vision in which God is presented as a severe judge and separate humans have different value even to Him - one group is always treated better than another.

Most clearly this limited understanding of the relationship between God and man is seen in the way that criminal law functions in all states around the world. The notion of a terrifying external power which enforces its law over people and which is inclined to throw them in unpleasant locations, if they do not obey is common understanding between many of the traditional religions and criminal legal systems of all countries.

---

2 *Principia, Book III*; cited in; Newton's Philosophy of Nature: Selections from his writings, p. 42, ed. H.S. Thayer, Hafner Library of Classics, NY, 1953

3 *The Expanded Quotable Einstein*, Princeton University Press, 2000 p.202

4 *My inventions*: Nikola Tesla's autobiography, 1919

Therefore, if we expect the emerging of new social models and intrinsic to them legal systems which are in the service to the whole, it is necessary that they correspond to much deeper comprehension of God. Such comprehension should support the building of harmonious relationships between all living beings, because they are finally perceived as unique manifestation of the divine Absolute.

The nascence of the holistic society is a result of applying of higher ideal for the divine power and more full understanding of the connection of every living being with the Absolute. The term "Absolute" is used to signify the unified divine power, which has created everything. It replaces the concept of an anthropomorphous God, who has a narrow perception of people and treats one person as his own and the others as foreign, a god who is trying to intimidate people and rudely impose his will over these creatures.

Every person represents a unique and significant manifestation of the Absolute who is equal with all other human-beings and who has an individual potential for spiritual development. This understanding directs us towards the attitude that the human can serve as a means for researching the whole and vice versa - the whole can serve for studying the human.

The presented common understanding of God should not lead to the conclusion that the holistic society is a closed religious organization or an emerging of a new religion. The basis for this statement is the fact that these ideals and understandings of the purpose of life we are finding in the logical and natural positive attitude towards life which leads to respectful treatment of everyone, including ourselves. Every major religion may find these ideals in its theory and probably discrepancies in their implementation in its practice.

It is of crucial importance that these understandings are clearly presented, because they serve as the basis for achieving unity between the participants in the process of building a society on the holistic model.

CHAPTER 2

THE HOLISTIC MODEL

Every society is built on the basis of a social model which identifies different subjects, defines their position in the system, hierarchical structure and legitimate legal interests. Every social order determines principles which generally regulate the relationships between individuals and collective entities. The formal embedding of these principles in the state is conducted by the law. Therefore, in order to understand the model, it is necessary to review several of the most important legal institutes.

The social model predetermines to a very high extend the attitudes of the participants towards themselves and everything else, which was briefly pointed out in the previous chapter. The model shapes the behavior of the participants in a very deep way. It serves more often as a catalyst of attitudes than as a natural result of already existing ones.

The creation of a new social model provides the opportunity to identify new subjects as well as conduction of a transformation of the relationships between already identified actors. This change is on a very deep psychological level and it brings with itself a new vision of the direction of social development, new priorities and adoption of new filters of world perception.

The holistic model considers all living beings as its subjects who are manifestations of the Absolute and part of the whole. It includes all relations that arise between them. The most efficient satisfaction of their interest is the most important designation of the holistic system.

It is important to note that the holistic community is equally responsible for human development and for the harmonious evolution of all other subjects of the holistic model, who are examined below. This characteristic illustrates that the holistic model is universal and exceeds just human relations. It is not just humanistic but also respectful for all life in general.

The necessity to identify the subjects in the frame of the whole is the first condition for proper satisfaction of their interests. Without differentiating them and without knowing them well, it is impossible to conduct rational action which aims to fulfill the needs of everyone in the system and to refine their environment.

Exhaustively we can define the following main subjects of the holistic model:

Humankind
Animals
Plants
Planet Earth
Extraterrestrial beings
Celestial bodies

The subjects of the holistic model should be constantly studied, because it is necessary their interests to be intertwined in such a way that they are optimally protected. Every existing bond between subjects and every activity should be considered in their variety, taking into account that they influence the whole environment. The planning of the activities in an organization, which functions according to the holistic model, is carrying out by finding the optimal way for mutual satisfaction of the interests of all subjects. These interests are arranged in hierarchical order, which will be examined below.

The holistic model embodies an ideology of respect of life and an attitude for cooperation between all living beings, so that the interest of the whole is satisfied in the best possible way. As a basic systemic model, it defines the principles and ground rules for the emerging and functioning of all future holistic organizations.

If we wend look back in the history, we will see that every positive social change in the world had come after protests, collective demands, organized movements and very often after many lost lives. This is evidence that until now the established political and social systems are conservative, stiff and with clumsy mechanisms for internal improvement.

The egoistic system perceives itself as a supreme and its participants as controlled resources. Therefore, the system, represented by its managers, does not consider it necessary to be improved and its governing methods and approach further developed. Every major positive change of state governance had come from bottom up, after refusal of participation and clearly formed requests from the governed people.

The holistic model is created with the aim of to avoid phenomenon like violation of rights, cultural decline, social degradation, dissatisfaction of participants from the system. To overcome these challenges, it is necessary to adopt clear working mechanisms for improving the holistic community. The most important condition for the efficiency of these mechanisms is to implement concrete criteria to determine when the direction of social development is better for the service of the whole and when it is worse than other options.

The most visible result from the efforts of developing the society is the economy. The economic basis of the holistic model corresponds to the principle of respectful treatment of living beings. It will be reviewed separately in chapter five and here we should only mention that it differs significantly from the known economic relationships in the capitalistic and the communistic systems.

The development and implementation of high technologies for proper functioning of the holistic community is important for its progress. However, greater focus is placed upon the development of spiritual and genetic potentials of the humans and all other living forms, as well as improving of the social relationships in the system, because they are the fundaments for protecting the interest of the whole. This spiritual evolution of the human, which includes the genetic bio-regeneration, is the leading path for development of the holistic society. This is a significant distinction from other movements and philosophies which stress on that technology should gradually replace biology.

In order organization to be holistic (in service to the whole) it should implement the holistic model, without regards how large it is and what is its management capacity. For example, one private corporation which has comparatively small capacity to include people, who would like to be part of it, should follow the same principles of holistic management, as well as a state which has chosen to function as a holistic organization. Therefore, it is irrelevant whether the number of people, participating in the organization, is a few, or hundreds of millions. If the principles and methods of the holistic model are applied, the organization shall function as a subject in the service to the whole.

Why the application of the holistic model is a prerequisite for the emerging of the holistic organizations?

The main reason is that in order to satisfy the interest of the whole, it is necessary to recognize the interests of all living beings as our own and not just to be respectfully considered. This attitude will lead to building of better functioning relationships between all participants. The holistic model is built in a way to avoid situations where a subject dominates and exploits other and turns him to be a victim.

From its name it becomes evident that this model is exhaustive and potentially capable to include all living organisms as participants of a unified system. The scope is of all living beings and their rights and freedoms are acknowledged. The interaction with others should be respectful and their interest protected in optimal way for the respective level of development of society.

The inclusion of all living beings is potential, because every particular holistic organization will determine its own capacity for inclusion of new participants, the conditions and level of their involvement. Every individual is free to choose to be part of a holistic organization, or not to be.

1. Subjects of the holistic model and participants in the holistic organizations

Comprehensive definition of the subjects of the holistic model is of crucial importance in order to form just and logic markers which interests are supposed to be protected simultaneously in a holistic organization.

There is an important distinction between the names "subjects of the holistic model" and "participants in a holistic organization". The first are generic terms on a level of planet and biological species - Earth, humankind, animals and plants. The second are the concrete representatives who are part of a holistic organization.

Earth and other celestial bodies are considered as separate subjects of the holistic model who have their own interests. By permeating of the outer space and potentially maintaining official contacts with extraterrestrial beings, the vast resources of outer space will become with

Scheme 1 - Subjects of the holistic model

even more value for the humankind than in the present. When this level of development is reached it is necessary the holistic model to include also the celestial bodies and the extraterrestrial beings.

The rights of the subjects of the holistic model serve as mandatory guidelines for all participants of holistic organizations. Depending on the type of the concrete organization, it may have different type of participants. If it is a private corporation which is an employer, its participants will be its employees. If the corporation own animals and plants, they also should be considered as participants and their rights have to be protected while harmonious relationships are built with external subjects.

If the holistic organization is a non-governmental with members, the participants will be precisely them.

If the holistic organization is a state, participants will be all private subjects with its citizenship, as well as all animals and plants which the state is responsible for. Presently, such private subjects are natural persons and all type of legal entities: companies, NGOs, religious organizations, etc. When are created new legal entities in a holistic organization, its objectives, organizational structure and functions should be in accordance with the aims and purpose of the holistic model. What we see today is that capitalistic states are regulating the activities of their private individuals. More details about the inner structure of a holistic organization are presented in chapter four.

In the holistic model all organizations, created by humans, without regard whether they are states, or private organizations, are in the scope of the primal subject - humankind. This means that their main interest and guideline for development shall be the interest of humankind. This requirement is derived from the logic conclusion that the state is an organizational structure of part of the humankind and therefore it is obliged not just to take it into consideration, but to satisfy it in the best possible manner.

The national interest should never be in conflict with the interest of humankind. Only then the holistic model can be adopted. Much to our regret this principle was constantly abused throughout all of the known history of polity, which will be briefly examined below.

The holistic model is presented in order to bring in the world an urgent change which could lead to harmonious development of humans from all nations.

Beside the private subjects, in the state there are also animals and plants which until present day are regarded as objects. In stark contrast, they are seen as indispensable subjects in the holistic model. Although animals and plants are not considered as legal subjects from the states (with the exception of dolphins from the side of India), they should be regarded as sentient beings, who are participants in the holistic organization and who have their own rights and legitimate interests.

1.1. Humankind - subject of the holistic model

The question "What is humankind?" at first seems trivial, perfectly obvious and unnecessary. However, if we examine deeper the popular hypothesis for origin of humans, we will stumble across inadequacy and vagueness. Presently are popular conjectures about the origins of life which are persuading us that humans have been primates and four billion years ago they even had a common ancestor with all other species, including with the plants. Today are publicly presented also ancient astronaut theories in which is described the population of Earth from representatives of different stellar races.

In order to define what humankind is, it is not enough to collect all known nations, tribes and civilizations from Ancient times until today. All social cultures on Earth are composed by humans and regulate human life, but it does not mean that their societies were acting congruently with the interest of humankind.

The cultural specifics of a tribe, nation or a civilization are an important historical heritage for the fact how this collective had treated humankind. It is evident from the social and religious norms, legal system, attitudes towards other people, who are foreigners, etc. Therefore there are two different and intertwined group subjects - the first is the nation, the second - humankind.

Consideration of humankind as a separate legal subject with its own legal interest is a comparatively new concept, which is a direct continuation of the process of humanizing the law and international relations in the last decades. This humanizing includes mainly the recognition that human have rights and freedoms and setting these principles as peremptory norms (jus cogens) in the legal systems of most states. Despite this positive direction of development of the civilization, the main driving force is still the service to self. The methods and means of organizing the state are in contradiction with the service to the whole and with abiding the interests of all participants.

What is the legal status of humankind presently?

In the contemporary international law we encounter the terms "humankind", "mankind" and "humanity" in few of the most prominent international treaties: The UN Charter; The Outer Space Treaty; The Convention of International Maritime Organization; The Antarctic Treaty; The Treaty on the Non-Proliferation of Nuclear Weapons; Convention Concerning the Protection of the World Cultural and Natural Heritage and others. Although the term "humankind" is used, there is not an official legal definition of it and what is in its legal significance.

Every group of people, without regards whether it exists as a legal entity or not, represents a manifestation of a specific community. It has its own social program which it desires to complete and its own interest which it protects. The group should be capable to organize its members and interacts with other groups in order to realize its objectives and fulfill its mission with which it is created.

On this basis, when we compare different groups of people, we clearly see that humankind is a primal group entity, without which could not emerge all social human structures including states, peoples, nations, religious organizations, companies, parties, universities, clubs, families, etc. Neither of these communities at this level of development can exist without humans. This means that the interest of humankind should be placed higher in the hierarchy of group interests in relation to the enumerated communities. This means that the actions of all them should not be in contradiction with the interests of humankind.

We can bring out the following definition of humankind:

Humankind is a primal group entity which includes all human beings, who have lived, are presently living, or who would be born in the future. Humankind perceives every human being as its unique manifestation, who is equally valuable with all others.

This definition provides the basic characteristics of humankind and leads to the important conclusion that the sum of all states and nations does not constitute humankind, does not have representative authority for humankind and cannot be an expression of the interests of humankind.

Neither the United Nations, nor the so called international community, nor any international organization, informal structure and, or state have the legal right to represent legally and politically humankind. Furthermore, until now neither of these subjects had declared that they will be compliant to the interests of humankind and they are violating it and ignoring it.

If we regard the UN as a legal subject, we see that it is an international organization in which national interests are cohered. The arithmetic sum of all national interests is not at equal to the interest of humankind. Typical examples for the disparity between the kind of interests(the total of all nations and the one of humankind) is the way the Earth environment is used, inhumane treatment of large groups of people, exploitation of natural resources without taking into consideration the future generations; waging wars between nations.

Concrete examples are the aims of the UN, which are described in the strategic document Millennium Development Goals. They set a target "to halve the proportion of the population without sustainable access to safe drinking water and basic sanitation". Such a target does not correspond with the holistic vision for humankind and demonstrates the weakness of the current international system of service to the self in which the national and corporate interests are pursued in violation of the interest of humankind.

From the view point of the humankind access to clean water is a basic need for all humans which should be satisfied anteriorly and before economic resources and human labor is used for any other purposes.

Achieving a specific proportion or statistically acceptable result which UN desires is not a measure for humanity which can be reliable or acceptable for humankind. It is because the death of people in misery, who do not have access to clean water, will be in favor of these statistics, but in contrast with the interest of humankind.

These goals of UN, which should be guiding for global governance of the world, demonstrate that the targets which this organization set are not necessarily in correspondence with the interest of humankind. More importantly, even if the targets of UN are humane, the UN does not have the authority and real competences to implement them or to exercise monitoring over their implementation. The UN serves only as a forum for discussions for the states and this means that qualitatively new legal organization is needed to represent humankind and its interest.

All states exploit the resources on their own territory as well as the resources which are common heritage of mankind (outer space and the seabed) depending on their own national policies of environmental protection of Earth and their development policies. The economic benefit from these resources are distributed on market principles which means that inequality is dominating and the future generations are not taken into consideration at all.

Another example of a significant contradiction between the national interests and the interest of humankind is the recourse to war for settling international disputes. From the view point of humankind every war is unacceptable and extremely undesirable, because humans are dying, without regards their citizenship, political views, religious believes, etc.

Scheme 2 - Humankind, countries, corporations

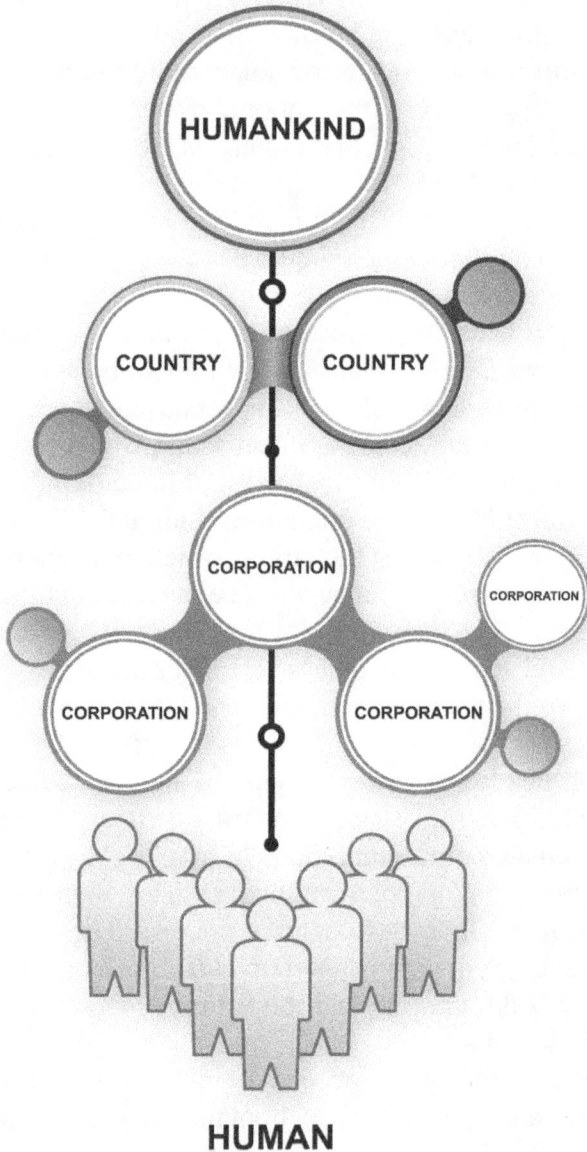

The definition of the humankind as a group entity which includes all human beings means that every human has a direct bond with it.

All races, ethnicities and nations which have existed and still exist can be perceived as important cultural and anthropologic aspects of humankind which create its diversity. Traditions and cultural specifics of certain societies can be evaluated according to how well they satisfy the human interests and how are seriously they were violating them.

For example societies in which slavery was institutionalized are incongruous with the humanistic ideals of humankind and their structures are in contradiction to human development. Without regards the economic, scientific, technological and military development of states, if their actions are inhumane, they are violating the interests of humankind.

From philosophical point of view humankind is clearly defined group entity and for everyone it is evident that it exists. From juridical point, however, arise two questions: "Is humankind a legal subject and can it become a legal subject?" The necessity a group entity to be a legal subject comes from the circumstance that it will protect in the best way its own interest and it has the right to be free, differentiated and represented. Only after its emerging as a legal subject, a group entity can appoint representatives who are supposed to protect its interests and to act on its behalf.

In order a community to be legally established, it should be able to have legal capacity and sui juris: to be able to express its will through its organ, to be capable to assume rights and obligations, including entering into treaties. Presently, because of the lack of such prerequisites, the humankind is not a subject of law.

In relation to the second question: "Can humankind become a legal subject", we should note that such a possibility do exist and at the same time it is much needed.

The legal "birth" of humankind should be via the establishment of organ which may be called: "Authority of humankind". It is important to stress that such an organ should be functioning as a holistic organization, which means taking into account and optimally protect the interests of the whole, including those of the other subjects of the holistic model.

The efforts to prevent all forms of possible ineffective functioning of the organ or misappropriation of official status of its representatives should be made before its establishing.

Differentiation of humankind as sovereign above-national legal subject will contribute significantly for the peaceful existence and prosperity of all nations, of all cultures, languages and humane cultural traditions.

The Authority of Humankind would not degrade the humane development of nations, but on the contrary - it will guarantee it. All military actions, forms of disrespect of human rights and economic subjugation of large groups of people are deeds not in the interests of humankind and of flourishing of national cultures. This is because the prosperity of every nation is possible only if is present a prosperity of the people in the corresponding state.

1.1.1. The human bond

The human bond is the fundament from which is shaped the concept of united humankind. This is the genetic bond between the individual and the group entity, thanks to which a person can be recognized as a human being. It exists, more precisely, it manifests from the moment a person is born and becomes a biological part of the human family. This bond gives us grounds to review humankind as a primary group entity. All races, ethnicities and nations are secondary in relation to humankind and can be regarded as its aspects. Because of the fact that before we are representatives of and race or nation, we are representatives of humankind and it is necessary all people to be aware of the bond which they do have with it. Through understanding of the nature of the human bond, the person is stimulated to know and respect the interests of all humankind.

We can compare the human bond with the citizenship which is another significant bond between the citizen and the state. In this comparison we will find that the last is secondary, because it is related to a secondary political organization which is the state and citizenship can be given, taken or abandoned under certain conditions. It is evident that a human being cannot be denied or refuse to have a human bond with a simple declaration, because it is genetic and therefore humankind - primary subject. Due to these specifics the legal interests of humankind should be recognized as such from a higher character with a priority of satisfaction over those of the state. This conclusion is very important in order to be able to see with different eyes - those of humankind, what it means two states to wage a war between them. This is an act of suicide from the view point of humankind.

The deliberation of the issue of the bond of the human with the humankind is especially topical when we see the fast development of biotechnologies and in particular the possibilities of human cloning and creation of hybrid individuals. Without any doubt we have to conclude that every cloned individual is equal and would have the same rights as all other human beings. Cloned individuals are/would be inseparable part of humankind.

Despite the fact that the Latin root of the word *homo* is related to the word *humus*, which mean "earth" and human beings literally means - "earthly beings" in the future humans may be born outside planet Earth. Such a possibility exists to some extend today too, considering the fact that presently people can dwell permanently space stations.

On theoretical level there is no doubt that human beings that would be born beyond Earth do possess a human bond, consequently are part of humankind and should be treated as equals to all other human beings. The relevant criterion is that a human is born from another human and has human genes, which means that there should not be a territorial principle, which limits humankind only to our planet.

The recognition of the human bond is necessary also from legal perspective, because it will clarify and systemize the system of human rights and we provide legal protection of all humans from infringement of these rights from states, private organizations or other humans. Precisely the legal recognition of the human bond will proclaim phenomena like slavery, war, death penalty, forced labor and other inhumane treatment as legally prohibited. It would not be necessary a nation to be evolved enough to respect all human rights, so that humane legislation start to emerge.

Would it be possible the newly adopted legal institute of the human bond to exist in parallel with the citizenship of a certain state?

If humankind is recognized as a legal subject with its organ which represents it and with its clearly defined legal interest which it aims to fulfill, then this will lead to the emerging of the legal institute of the human bond.

The existence of states as political organizations parallel with the Authority of Humankind requires the human bond to be acknowledged as a legal institute that is side by side with citizenship. Presently, it is possible a human being to have more than one citizenship, which provides him with rights and duties to more than one state.

The recognition of the human bond will lead to granting larger package of human rights with which every state will have to conform. The basic argument for recognizing humankind as above national legal subject, which stands higher than all states and which interests are with priority over all national interests, is in the fact that the human bond is primary for the human being, while citizenship is secondary.

The legal institute of the human bond would contribute to be solved the legal ineffectiveness and disorder when there are violations of human rights. Presently, one state may choose whether to sign and ratify an international treaty for human rights, to determine which rights will be protected and which may not be. The institute of the human bond, respectively the emerging of humankind as a legal subject, would regulate human rights as obligations that states have to representatives of humankind and not to their citizens, or foreign citizens. These obligations would not come from its legislation and absence of ratifications or internal legislation cannot be an excuse for human rights violation.

Another strong argument for the higher status of humankind in relation to states and corporations is that it includes all human beings and its historical roots go beyond the history of any nation or private subject. In modern days states cannot function without representatives of humankind, while humans have lived and would be able to in other organizational forms, which are not necessarily states.

1.1.2. Future and past generations of humankind

In the definition of humankind are included also human beings, who were living in the past and those who might be born in the future.

The inclusion of past generations in the scope of humankind means, in the first place, that it is necessary to take actions through which to be objectively researched the history of humankind, to be protected the cultural and historic heritage and access to this information to be freely provided to everyone.

Secondly, the historical review will help to draw important conclusions on issues like ill functioning states and religious organizations are trampling on human rights and oppressing freedoms and knowledge. These conclusions will help humanity to get rid of such primitive and inhuman organizational models.

The research and protection of historical and cultural heritage does not necessarily mean that the respective groups of people were acting in the interest of humankind. Turning back to history we see how many wars, bloodshed and other form of inhumane aggression was done from most tribes and nations, but this does not mean that the memory for them should not be preserved.

Knowing and rationalizing the flaws and achievements of the past generations is inseparable part of the development of the civilization and is an important component of the interest of humankind.

The right of a human being to know his origins and history should be recognized as legally protected human right. Respectively, hiding of historical facts and events, as well as, their deliberate incorrect presentation and interpretation, are acts in violation of the interest of humankind. Such actions should be prohibited to be performed by all states and eventually by the future Authority of Humankind.

The future generations are also part of humankind and this should be taken into account by a future organ in the process of formulating the interest of humankind. This means that exploitation of resources in a way which is beneficial for humans and for the environment should be also performed in long term plan with the aim to be left sufficient resources for the future generations, but also for all other subjects of the holistic model. Long term planning, which includes also the future generations, is key principle for developing of branches like ecology, planetary management of resources and protection of cultural and natural heritage of humankind, preservation of Earth and reasonable exploitation of outer space.

Through this vision of other generations are created bridges between past, present and future. In this way we can understand more fully the interest of humankind and to set a balance rhythm of social development in which every person could have the opportunity to live happily and freely. Happiness is a personal choice and internal condition, but the favorable outer environment and maintenance of harmonious social relationships can be instrumental for achieving this goal and a right of every person. Placing the individual happiness of humans as a goal in front of the community, is important, if this community desires to manage its resources efficiently. These resources will be used to protect the rights and satisfy the needs of all its members equally.

1.1.3. The interest of humankind

The clear defining of the interest of humankind is of crucial importance in order to be placed the right aims and to set the principles and methods for their realization. In its scope are included those values which are fundamental for humanism. For example, from the view point of humankind all human beings are its equally important manifestations and therefore the right to live should be protected for all people, including those who are committing crimes and inhumane deeds. The using of military force against people should be a last resort action which is again violation of the interest of humankind. It would be reasonable to adopt global legal mechanisms to guarantee that all international disputes will be solved peacefully.

We can bring out a few of the main principles which are an integral part of the interest of humankind:

All human beings are equally important manifestation of humankind and possess equal human rights, including economic.

Humankind should have the resources to guarantee the protection of the human rights of everyone, without regards his/her citizenship, gender, race, economic status or any other features.

Humankind should encourage the use of humane methods for interaction with every human being who will be introduced with the interest of humankind and the opportunity to recognize them as his own.

Humankind aims to provide more favorable environment for development of the future generations.

Humankind is obligated to research its history and make it freely available to everyone.

Humankind perceives Earth as a planet with which it has special connection. Extraction and use of its resources should be performed in ecological way which protects the interest of the Earth, the animals and the plants.

The exploration and exploitation of outer space, including all celestial bodies should be executed in a way which is not harmful for their ecosystem and integrity. The resources from outer space are already recognized for province of all mankind and should be used in a way which protects in the best way the interests of humankind.

With the emergence of humankind as a legal subject, it should be legally acknowledged that its interest is superior to those of all national and corporate interests. It is because, at this level of development states cannot function without humans and it is the sovereign right of the last to organize themselves and establish an Authority of humankind and demand human rights protection from all states.

The way a corporation is obligated to conform its behavior to the relevant national legislation, the states should comply their national policies towards human beings without violating the principles set by the organ which is representing humankind. The result of such compliance will be that all national interests will be legitimate and permissible if they do not violate the interest of humankind.

Achieving a level of consciousness that before we are citizens of a certain state, we are human beings, who have common appurtenance with all others is possible only after personal efforts and free conviction and cannot be a vision, imposed over anyone.

Clarification of the service to humankind and of the obligations of states should not be considered as unpatriotic and derogatory attitude towards national interests. On the contrary, humanity is already recognized globally as essential thread for adopting a national interest. The recognition of humankind as superior legal subject to the state is also a civil position for the development of the society.

Presently are absent the clear criteria for determining of the national interests and states are competing with ostensible threads and named enemies on national and international level, instead of being focused on improving the life of representatives of humankind.

All organizational forms of people should formulate their interest without violating the interest of humankind, if human beings who are related with these organizations declare that they are acknowledging the Authority of humankind as representative organ. This is valid for all states, international organizations, corporations and other private organizations.

The creation of an Authority of humankind would be a major shift in international relations, because human beings would be finally represented. Major conflicts may be solved and not exploited for egoistic national and corporate interests.

Such an organ would not be burdened with one-sided civilizational ties with certain states or religions, but it will be responsible to protect the interest of all humankind and to contribute for the peaceful solving of international disputes.

The next important competency that the organ should have is related to ownership of patents to inventions and the obligation to facilitate their free use in the interest of humankind. Even today such inventions and technologies do exist, which could be easily introduced to all people and which will result in improving the quality of their life and their health.

1.2. Animals - subject of the holistic model

The relationships between humans, animals and plants are one of the most complicated areas for finding a balance in satisfying their interest, so that the interest of the whole is optimally protected. Part of this complexity comes from the fact circumstance that humans and animals are forced to consume other biological species, in order to guarantee their own survival. Therefore, to suffice the needs of these large groups of subjects, it is absolutely necessary to research thoroughly their relations.

Placing all animal species in one large group is a large generalization and it requires further investigation and systematization of the interests of the separate subspecies. The description of the holistic model includes presentation of the relationships on a global level between humankind, animal, plants and the Earth.

If the interest of humankind is reviewed detached from the interests of the other subjects of the holistic model, this will mean that animals, plants and the Earth will be exploited only as objects which have different value to humans. They will continue to be used for purposes and with means which human beings desire and they would not have any rights whatsoever. Unfortunately, this type of thinking is predominant for thousands of years and it creates many problems for every being on the planet. Such rights are necessary to be adopted not just for preservation of biological species, but also for drastic improvement of their treatment.

What does it mean to defend the interests of animal species in a way which does not violate the interests of humankind?

In order to reply accordingly to this question, it is necessary to stand out what do we know about these two subjects of the holistic model and to regard what are the relationships that different animal species do have with human beings.

The relationships between the subjects are determinative for the quality of development of any social system and from the way that they are structured shows whether it is an egoistic or a holistic one. The same participants exist in both system, but the recognition of the rights and interests of all of them as important and the building of harmonious relationships between them will provide the fundaments for much balanced development of this society.

The relationships and bonds between human beings and animal species are well known: some animals are used for food, with others is adopted a bond of irreplaceable companionship; third have played an important role in areas like transport, work force, communication, entertainment, medicine and even espionage. In order to be satisfied the interest of the whole, it is necessary in the process of forming and developing of any relationship to be reached an optimal level of protection of the rights of all involved subjects. Detailed researches for improving these relationships through the use of holistic approach are needed to be conducted in future investigative works. Below will be briefly reviewed how to determine the relationship between animals which are food resources for human beings and animals, because this is the most serious violation of rights of those species.

Large groups of animals are presently used as a needed food resource for humankind and this condition should be clarified to what extend is absolute, so that people are fed and healthy. The movements of vegetarianism and veganism are indicative that meat consumption is not absolutely necessary for all. The criteria on this issue are individualized for every person in order to establish which good is healthy for him and what kind of food he would like to consume. The supporters of these movements will point out that if it is possible for a few, it should be possible for the others too. Those people that enjoy eating meat will state arguments that it is their right and that they are obtaining nutrients for their organisms.

It has to be noted that eating plants is also a process which deserves to be organized in way, which is respectful of their interests. Presently, it is not popular to see plants as beings, whose interests should also be protected during the process of eating, but the holistic model includes them too in the global picture.

From a holistic point of view it is important to recognize who the affected species are and how their interests to be violated in the least possible way.

The legal interest of animals can be described most comprehensively by the people who are aware most about the particular species. It is already scientifically proven uncontrovertibly that certain animals can communicate with humans. Therefore, it is logical to accept that these beings should have the right to participate in the process of describing their interest. This thesis is unpopular in the legal philosophy, because large parts of the humankind could not concede the idea that there are animal species that are intelligent beings with their own individuality. An example of such beings is the dolphins for which it is already established that they communicate through a complicated sono-pictorial language. Dolphins are capable to communicate with human beings on a high level and possess the capabilities to take decisions in complicated situations.[5]

In some of the national legal systems, for example those of New Zealand, is already foreseen that animals should be treated as sentient beings. This means that their sensitivity is recognized, as well as the capability to feel positive and negative emotions.[6]

These legal activities of a state set the grounds for adopting the legal interests of different animal species and this means clarifying

_____

5 More information about the language of dolphins and researches about the complexity of their communication see: http://www.speakdolphin.com
6 Animal Welfare Amendment Act(No2), 2015, Date of assent 09.05.2015

what is positive and harmonious for their development and what is not. Human beings are responsible for the good life of animals. This is an important task for humankind and all organizational structures have to improve the interaction between humans and animals, so that it is beneficial for both.

In the scope of the interest of animals it is logical to include their right to be treated respectfully as beings, which deserve dignified life and pleasant environment. In order their interest to be satisfied even better, it is necessary to draw out much more improved and concrete measures for decent living of animals. The needed resources for implementing these measures will be defined by humankind, without significant infringing of its interest.

The first condition for satisfaction of the interest of animals is to determine which beings will be consumed and how many of them. They have to be in a quantity which doesn't threaten the entire species from extinction. Appropriate measures should be taken to preserve all biological species. The attitudes towards the other animals should not be depreciating, but caring and devoted.

The next important step is to preserve their genetic heritage. When humankind is not fully aware what would be the consequences of conducting genetic manipulations to the health of the animal or of the person, who is going to consume it, such experiments should not be performed. The scientific researches in the fields of genetics and microbiology are in their initial stage and if they are not undertaken with great care and with respect to life, they could be detrimental for biological species and cause irreparable damages.

The third step is to provide pleasant and conducive environment for all animals, including to those that are determined to be consumed. This means that they should have normal life span, living space, healthy food and to be optimally reduced all forms of stress and pain.

In relation to the animals which will be killed in to be used as a resource by humans or other animals, if we approach this act from the perspective of their interest, it should be conducted in the least painful and stressful manner. Presently, such measures are not implemented from meat producers, because they are seen as unjustified costs. More information about the modern treatment of animals from the meat industry corporations are presented in chapter five.

Lastly, the economic process should be organized in such a way that as few animals as possible should be killed.

The practicing of a holistic approach for decision making in the interest of all means that the factors and conditions for better protection of the interest of animals are dynamic and developing. At the same time they are intertwining with the interest of humankind and are limited by it. The measures for improving life of animals should not be an excessive burden for humankind, because the interest of humankind is considered with priority in the holistic system over interest of animals and plants. The holistic system should adopt criteria and indicators which integrate in the best way all affected group interests. For example, the living space, conditions and food for the animals should be provided without this to violate the living conditions and food of human beings.

There is a difference between acknowledging the legal interest of animals and recognizing them as legal subjects. In order for someone to be recognized as a legal subject, which means to have the ability to acquire rights and obligations, it is a prerequisite for him to take decisions and being able to express his own will. Therefore, firstly, this being should be able to form an attitude towards the world, distinguishing himself as an individual and secondly - to be able to express his intention to interact with the others. When these prerequisites are present, it is possible for this being to be recognized as a legal subject.

The modern day egoistic civilization needed thousands of years to start acknowledging all human individuals as legal subjects, who are relevantly free and citizens with rights. Considering that humanism and spiritual attitude towards life are not guiding principles for present day society and it still is primitive in this sense, is it logical to expect that modern society will treat animals as beings which have legitimate legal interest? For most of the political leaders such question is not only irrelevant, but also distractive of "more important" issues such as economic prosperity of part of humankind at the expense of others.

Among the presented prerequisites for having a legal personality, purposefully is not included the ability of the being (in this case animal) to be understood by human. The reason is that it is a subjective criterion which is refers to abilities, attitudes and the willingness of human beings to learn to communicate and this should not affect the rights of animals. The fact that humans established in the last decades what the language of dolphins is does not mean that this communication could not have emerged potentially thousands of years ago. The breakthrough in communication with other intelligent beings is happening when representatives of humankind are developed enough and open enough for this interaction.

When human beings accept the fact that they do not know fully the other biological species and even themselves then it would be possible for raising awareness of humankind, accumulating knowledge and developing more complex relationships with others. Until this happens, it is not justifiable other intelligent species to be treated as senseless objects and their interests to be violated.

When human beings are respectful towards other biological species and recognize their legal interest, then will be reached better understanding of them on the side of humankind.

The adoption of the holistic model means that animals are treated firstly as conscious beings which are manifestation of the Absolute and after that some of them - as needed resource for human beings and other animals. This worldview differs significantly from all legal systems which have existed from Ancient times until modern days.

Treating animals as sentient beings is the first step on the road of acknowledging them as legal subjects, because it is recognized that they do have senses, emotions and the right to live happy.

Such issues may seem distant and not significant for many of the modern day people, because in their daily agenda is deliberately placed and maintained the problem of their personal survival. The solution of all egoistic systems is this survival to be at the expense of everyone else - humans, animals, plants or planets, while the person sells his labor force for activities which are not necessarily useful and beneficial for others.

The holistic model proposes the building of much more harmonious relationships between all subjects of the holistic model (all living beings) and encouraging of attitudes which are widening the consciousness of the participants to the point that they feel themselves as unique part of the whole.

In the particular issue of building the relationships between humans and animals, as much it is filled with love and respect, as more developed both species will be.

1.3. Plants - subject of the holistic model

If the rights of the animals are a topic, which gathers many supporters and is present in the legal regulation of states, it is not popular to think that plants also are entitled to rights, should have their own legal interest and deserve respectful treatment. As animals are placed in a very general group of one subject, which needs further classification, so are the plants, which are considered as one group of living organisms and a subject of the holistic model. It also has to be researched in detail and separate types of plants further studied and classified.

Neurobiologists, who are investigating different plants, determine not only that they are intelligent beings, but also that some species possess at least twenty different senses, which are tracking different changes in their environment.[7] The authors of these scientific findings place a particular focus on the fact that cultural prejudices and human arrogance are leading to underestimation and negligence of these complex living organisms.

In the holistic model of social organizing should be defined and regarded the legitimate rights of plants as living organisms. This means that the preservation of specific plant species is conducted with the aim of its prosperous living and this is a principle of every organization which implements the holistic model. The need to use some of the plants as a resource for the living of animals and humans is a secondary feature which is important for those species that need them. The legal interests of plants are part of the interest of the whole and in the holistic model they will be placed in a specific hierarchy in relation to the other subjects. Such hierarchy is necessary to exist, in order to resolve the imminent collision of interests between species.

Plants should be considered as species on a lower level than animals, which means when there is unsolvable collision of interests, at the corresponding moment, with priority will be those of animals.

Modern science is making experiments with the genetics of living organisms in a way which, from a holistic point of view, violates the rights of these beings and threatens their natural existence. When the existence of a participant in an ecosystem is endangered, are threatened also the life of the others and is initiated a chain reaction of problems

---

7 Stefano Mancuso and Alessandra Viola; *Brilliant Green: The surprising history and science of plant intelligence*, Island Press, 2015

for the whole system. Many of the participants in these egoistic systems are aware of these results, but they ignore the solution because of selfish motives such as bigger profit and maintenance of dependence of the consumers from a specific resource. The holistic approach requires not only consideration of the problem, but also its cardinal solution through improvement of the relationships between participants in a direction, which is optimally beneficial for their development.

What would happen if it is recognized that plants have legal rights?

Firstly, this would mean that it is required a serious rethinking of the whole ecologic and economic cycles of living of the species, so that the way that they are preserved is permanently improving. As was mentioned above, plants are used by humans as a basic resource for food, clothes, medicine, construction, furniture, paper and many other economic branches. The recognition of rights would not lead to starvation of animals and humans, or ceasing of the existence of the other areas of life in which they are used. It will result in selected breeding of plant species, for which is determined to be used as economic resources. Protecting their rights means also that such breeding should be conducted with a sense of great respect and attitude towards them as living beings which are part of the whole and unique manifestations of the Absolute.

The main conclusion from recognizing of the rights of the plants is that humankind will devote much more efforts, resources and attention for the care and protection of all species. When it is necessary some to be used as resources, this should not threaten their kind from extinction.

Even though that plants are a different class of living organisms than animals, the basic principles for respectful interaction, which were already mentioned above, should be used for both groups. This includes in the first place determining which species shall be used as economic resource. Those species should be in such quantity which does not threaten the whole kind from extinction.

The second principle is to preserve the natural genetic characteristics of a plant. When the results of genetic modifications remain unknown for the concrete organism, such should not be conducted.

Another principle which protects the interests of the plants is the optimal organization of the production process and particularly the reducing of non-used resources.

The preservation of all species, the formulation and regard of their legal interest requires that plants should be researched thoroughly by humankind. This means that the holistic organization should devote significant efforts and resources for implementing the activities that protect the interests of plants.

This policymaking focus on preserving all species is much bigger in the holistic society than in the modern-day environmental policies of the self-service capitalistic systems.

1.4. Extraterrestrial beings - subject of the holistic model

The existence of an intelligent life beyond Earth is an issue, which noticeably excites a large part of humankind in our days. For many researchers of extraterrestrial life there are already available solid evidences that non-terrestrial beings do exist and even more that contact with them was already made by individuals and by representatives of governments on Earth. The conviction of these researchers, among which is the author of this book, is that these contacts are not publicly disclosed and acknowledged by representatives of governments, because this will require vast and deep changes of the structures of our society and providing of answers of tough questions that people would have. The holistic model provides the opportunity provides the opportunity to answer in a humane way to the challenges, which will emerge, when every human being on planet is fully aware that humans are not alone in outer space and on Earth.

For the other still large part of the humankind, who are skeptical and not sharing the view that contact with extraterrestrials have been made, the legal status of non-terrestrial beings, as subjects of the holistic model, may by perceived hypothetically, as a mental exercise. We should not forget that the statement that "there are no intelligent extraterrestrial individuals" is methodologically incorrect, because it affirms an absence of something which is in the early steps of investigation, like the presence of life in our Milky Way galaxy. Everyone who is making such a statement, including a scientist or a politician, is correctly to reformulate it to "I am not aware about the existence of extraterrestrial beings". Every other statement is disrespectful to all of the society and reveals an unhealthy intention for maintaining ignorance among people and misguiding the public opinion from the serious research and evaluation of facts.

Similarly to the presented criteria for determining of the legal status of animals and plants on Earth, it is logical that these principles and methodology are relevant for the extraterrestrial life. If there is life, it should be approached with respect and with regard to its legitimate interests. If it is established that this being has the capacity to take decisions and to be aware of its own individuality, it should be granted legal status and respected its sovereign right to choose its own path of development.

Unlike animals and plants, some extraterrestrial beings may be much more advanced from the human in technological and spiritual sense.

The inclusion of extraterrestrial beings as part of the holistic model means that it is necessary to be made a detailed evaluation of their legal interests and also their influence to humankind and the whole in general, if interaction is established. In this regard, precisely the united humankind is appropriate to be the legitimate subject that is interacting with extraterrestrials with representative authority and not states or international organizations. The reason is that the last are following their own national interests and are often neglecting the interests of humankind and those of the whole. If contemporary subjects of law are acting with more developed extraterrestrial beings, this could lead to inhumane deed towards own citizens or foreign one in pursue of strategic military and scientific advantage.

By considering extraterrestrial beings as subject of the holistic model, we should make an important distinction with animals and plants on Earth. It consists of the fact that humans are responsible for the development of other biological species on the planet and at the same time for their own prosperity. Such bond and obligations do not exist automatically in the case of interaction with extraterrestrial beings, because they are (could be) independent from humankind and sovereign individuals. Humankind has the right to choose whether to interact with them and how to communicate with such beings, but it has the responsibility to protect animals and plants on Earth. Therefore, the most important characteristic of the contact with intelligent extraterrestrial beings and their potential inclusion among the subjects of the holistic model is to determine very carefully what would be the impact for humankind, animals, plants and Earth, from the interactions with the corresponding beings.

It cannot be overstated that the necessity of multilayered preliminary analysis of such contact with extraterrestrial beings is of crucial importance for protection of the interests of humankind and of the whole!

1.5. Earth - subject of the holistic model

In the holistic model Earth and other celestial bodies are regarded as conscious and highly-developed living beings which are among the subjects. From a scientific point such a hypothesis is not fully proven until now, but its acceptance as a postulate will bring to many positive attitude and actions towards our planet.

An important conclusion of considering Earth as a subject of the holistic model is that its protection and preservation is conducted for its own sake, and not only because of the need to adopt efficient resource management policies for humans and other beings.

For example, if it is established that certain natural resources (like gold, oil or gas) are vitally needed for the harmonic existence of Earth and their mining and drilling has a harmful effect over the planet, this circumstance should be taken into account and production activities mitigated or even prohibited.

All tests of nuclear weapons, hydrogen bombs, stockpiling of radioactive waste, can be categorized as action, which are harmful to Earth. The environmental and energy policies of humankind have to be consistent with the interests of Earth. Ideally, all activities which are dangerous for the planet should be banned.

The preservation of Earth as an environment for all other living beings is also of key importance for the development of the holistic system, and is placed as a leading principle for developing of holistic organizations. Our planet is needed environment also of the future generations of humankind and other biological species, which means that its use should be very well planned.

Holistic organizations will place much more attention and resources towards preservation of Earth, than these are performed nowadays.

Global holistic planning of the economy, elimination of the competition between organizations, when the case is of using public property, will lead to firm, balanced and ecological use of Earth's natural resources, which is absent in the capitalistic and communistic systems.

The inclusion of our planet as part of the holistic model means that holistic organizations will have to take into consideration what is beneficial for the planet and what is less harmful for it in the planning of all economic processes.

1.6. Celestial bodies - subjects of the holistic model

In the contemporary international space law is proclaimed that „… *celestial bodies, is not subject to national appropriation by claim of sovereignty, by means of use or occupation, or by any other means*"[8], and also that they are *"province of all mankind"*[9]. When is acknowledged the existence of intelligent extraterrestrial life, it will be logical to be made changes of the legal status of the celestial bodies, which should not be regarded as a province only for human beings from Earth.

If humankind is recognized as a legal subject with its own juridical authority, this would be a major step in the development of space law and an opportunity to solve many challenges, which exist until today. Some of these unresolved issues are: absence of legal delimitation between airspace and outer space; absence of unified standards for launching of space objects; absence of unified planetary quarantine protocol for back contamination; lack of legal obligation to preserve outer space environment from different types of space debris; failure to use the resources of outer space in the interest of humankind and to replace the principle "first come, first served". Another major issue which is not presently resolved is positioning of space objects on the principle "the most suitable orbit" from the perspective of humankind and not in the interest of private corporations and states.

The treating of celestial bodies as subject of the holistic model, which has its own legal interest is important for the future development of holistic organizations on Earth. It is because the resources for investigative missions of other planets and the approach of conducting those activities should not violate their ecosystem and entirety. A holistic or-

---

8 Art.2 of the Outer Space Treaty, 1967
9 Art.1 of the Outer Space Treaty, 1967

ganization is not supposed to harshly exploit outer space and to explore it in relation to its own interest, but it will have to act as a guardian of the celestial bodies and the life on them, if such exists.

When are implemented policies for conducting exploration and exploitation of outer space, they should be coherent with the holistic methods and approaches for prevention of damage to the outer space environment in general and celestial bodies in particular.

States are still the main subjects of law and they are pursuing egoistically their national interests. In relation to outer space, this results in its dangerous contamination and threat of life of astronauts and people on Earth. Presently, the direction of development of exploration and exploitation of outer space is in drastic violation of the interest of humankind. The absence of international legal guarantees that the results of all activities in outer space will be timely and fully announced to the public turns it in a competitive and hostile environment for states and private organizations.

The strive of leading states to demonstrate military space potential has included the execution of hundreds of antisatellite tests, which lead to irrecoverable pollution in the actively used lower-Earth and medium-Earth orbits. The negative effect of these actions is that in the regions, where space debris is formed by the fragments of destroyed satellites, it will not be possible to place a functional space object. The already placed objects will be threatened from destruction in future collisions.

With the eventual growing of the number of the holistic organizations, the competition between their participants would be gradually removed and replaced with a mentality of cooperation for the benefit of the whole. This will lead to much better project management and global planning of the use of satellites and other space objects for the need of all subjects of the holistic model. Another result of eliminating of competition will be the free flow of information and the resources for militarization against others will be transferred for scientific projects for the benefit of all humankind.

Through the affirmation and grounding of the holistic model in different states, it would be possible to implement much more ecological policies in outer space activities, which are respectful to the whole.

The inclusion of celestial bodies among the other subjects of the holistic model is essential, in order to be taken into consideration what is happening in outer space, even when are conducted activities on Earth. In the near future, in the first half of this century, this mindset will be absolutely needed precondition for achieving good governance and just use of the resources of outer space on Earth. They will become much more used in the global economy, than they are in present days.

2. Hierarchy of the legal interests

Every subject has its own interests, which he aims to achieve and to protect. When they are considered as important enough for society and the state, the interests become legitimate and legal. Then they are placed interrelated with the interests of others and put in a hierarchical order.

The methods and means for achieving one's interest are regulated by the law through the adoption of different requirements, limitations and incentives. The holistic approach aims not only to limit the harmful impact of a subject over another, but also to organize and synchronize the actions of all participants in a way to achieve optimal satisfaction of their interests and from - that the interest of the whole. In order this to happen, it is necessary to raise the awareness of the individuals towards understanding the unity and the purpose of community building in the service of the whole. This society will create equal benefits for all its members and will free itself from economic privileges and social stratification, based on ownership.

Nowadays it is not popular to distinguish a hierarch of legal interests of the separate subjects, even though that bringing clarity on this issue will outline much better the social functions of everyone in society. When we use the term "hierarchy", it does not mean that one subject is more important than another, but it means that for the interest of the subject below there is a due form of compliance with the interest of the subject above. It is necessary in order to solve global challenges from a higher perspective and with the least possible harm of the interests of all subjects. For example, we may define that the interest of humankind are with priority and stand above than those of animals. In the holistic model, and for the build on it holistic organizations, every subject are considered equally important parts of the whole, which are on a different path of their evolution.

As it is not necessary to compare which organs of our body are more important than others, because every organ has its unique functions for our harmonious life, so the subjects of the holistic model have their unique purpose and place to benefit the whole. Every subject in the holistic society should be perceived as an organ in a larger organism.

Hierarchy of the legal interest exists also in the systems of service to self. In contemporary legislation is envisaged juxtaposition of the interests of the state and the private persons and priority is foreseen for the state's interest. For example, in the legislation of every country is foreseen the right of the state to expropriate for its own benefit any private property, if certain conditions are met and most of the time after equal compensation.[10] It is a normal practice and a justified legal principle among modern states.

This fundamental norm illustrates that all legal subjects are in a specific hierarchical interrelation and the exercising of their freedom is regulated by rules, set by a higher legal authority. It is evident in the functioning of the state government in which organs of the state are defining the legal norms on its territory and the rules which are supposed to regulate all private subjects. The state has the authority to change the legal regime of private ownership, to confiscate it, implementing rules, which are set by it, but the opposite is impossible. There is not a legal barrier a state and a private organization to be in a relationship as equal subjects, for example when they are signing a treaty. Despite this equality, the legal instruments for impact, including the creation of compulsory norms on the side of the state, give the ground to review the interests of private subjects standing on a lower level than those of the state.

Hierarchy of the legal interests we see also in the private relationships. Corporation may create its legal branches, which are its subordinates and are functioning under its management.

In relation to the provision of labor force to a private corporation and hiring of employees, it is fair to regard the relationship between employer and employee not in hierarchy, but in the sense of managerial influence. The corporation possesses certain authority over its employee and this is seen in its obligation to adopt internal labor rules which

---

10 In the case of Bulgaria such norm is postulated in article 17(5) of the Constitution of Republic of Bulgaria.

are compulsory for the employee, determines their work and remuneration. The corporation is capable to change the vital access to finances, respectively to goods for its employee.

It is important to be aware about the hierarchy in which all participants are in a system, if we want to understand which interests are with a priority for satisfaction over others and should be abided by all participants.

Contemporary international relations have come to the stage in which every state in theory can be sovereign and it can be unacceptable any state to impose its will over others. If a state freely declines from its sovereignty and is dominated by another, it is the choice of the first, for which it is responsible. At the same time, presently there are not any efficient legal mechanisms for encouraging observation of human rights: i.e. observing the interests of humankind. There aren't also any working mechanisms for preserving the planetary environment and to regulate a balance use of outer space in the interest of humankind.

In the holistic model are introduced and openly presented the hierarchy of interests, which aims to clarify the functions of different subjects, the direction and limitation of exercising their freedom.

3. Building relationships between the subjects of the holistic model

After the enumeration and brief description of the subjects of the holistic model, it is necessary to review the relationships between them and to answer the question how to improve them, so that the system of the service to the whole functions even better.

Soaring of relationships between all subjects is a constant process which depends on many factors: discovery of new subjects; implementation of new inventions; broadening of knowledge of already known subjects; positive or negative changes in the environment and others. The guiding principle of improving these relationships is: better protection of the interest of the whole through optimal satisfaction of the needs of all subjects.

The holistic model is not static and is constantly developing. This is related with the level of broadening of human awareness about the world and also about the universe and cosmos.

How can we respect the interests of so many individuals and collectives? Can we satisfy the needs of humankind and all animals and plants, while protecting Earth and the celestial bodies and at the same time take into account the future generations, which might not even be born?

The answer is that through the application of a holistic approach and seeking of mutually satisfactory solutions, humankind will manage to understand and protect its interest, those of other subjects and in the end - of the whole.

When we know which the subjects of the holistic model are and what is their interest in general, we have to describe the relationships between them and to aim their permanent improvement. This description does not aim to dogmatize their relationships or to place limitations towards exercising their free will. The importance of portraying the relationships comes from the fact the need to understand life more fully and cultivate respect towards it. The main types of relationships can be classified in, according to three criteria:

1. Relationships between fellow subjects of the holistic model, who are living at the same time;

2. Relationships between various subjects of the holistic model, who are living at the same time;

3. Trans-time relationships between subjects

An example of the first type of relationships is those between humans in the present. Contemporary legal systems regulate them and as a result they do not take into consideration of all humankind and are ignoring many groups of people for the benefit of small exploitive elite. There are many examples from the past until present day that human relations have been distorted and inequality had been maintained, so that people are used as a resource in competitive struggle for survival.

Modern states do not support many of the cases of inhumane treatment and foresee harsh sanctions in their criminal justice and penal systems. In other cases, on the other side, the inhumane treatment is disregarded by the state and it is perceived as normal situation in certain community for the relevant historical period.

For example, in modern days many of the stated accept as a legal and valid attitude from their point to take human lives through death penalty for a specific crime. Other examples for violation of the interest of humankind from all states without exception is the maintaining of unequal access to goods and services for citizens of the same state through implementing economic division; concealing information for important events; deprivation of rights to clean environment and others.

The second type of relationships regulates the bonds between different subjects of the holistic model. These relations are between humankind and Earth; humankind and animals; humankind and plants; animals and plants; animals and Earth; plants and Earth.

When new subjects are emerging (discovery of new animal or plant species; taking possession of a new planet; contact with extraterrestrial beings) the relationships with them should also be taken into consideration and properly integrated to the holistic model. All of these relationships require a thorough research not only in relation to the directly affected subjects, but also to the impact of the whole system. As was mentioned above, the relationships should always be developed and the criterion for an improvement is the better service to the whole. The building of harmonious relations between different types of subjects will lead to substantial transformation of the economic processes, because completely different objectives will be pursued than in present days. This understanding will give an impulse for the emergence of a new type of economic, which can be called holistic. More information about it is presented in chapter five.

The third type of relationships is trans-time. In them the subjects are from different time periods. In the process of reviewing these bonds the focus is placed on past and future generations of all subjects of the holistic model. An example is the planning to use the resources of Earth in a way which can be satisfied the interests of the future generations of humankind, animals and plants, and preserved the heritage of the past generations. Taking into consideration the trans-time relationships between subjects is of crucial important for the implementation of the holistic model and good governance of a holistic organization. Typical for egoistic systems is the neglecting of these bonds in the maintenance of the contemporary capitalistic economy and in spending of resources for preservation of all species.

The lack of understanding of the trans-time relationships leads to inability to adopt good practices and to mismanagement of social processes. A typical example of weak trans-time civilizational relationships is disregarding of achievements of a past historical period. This we can see during the coming of the Middle Ages in Western Europe and the sharp deterioration of the hygiene of the people, as if there were no baths, aqueducts and other irrigation facilities in the times of the Roman Empire.

In present days, even if there are cheap measures for building of long-term positive results to preserve biological species, states and corporations are not obliged to apply them. Egoism is an attitude which is blindsiding the senses and when a person performs a harmful behavior to the environment or observes others to do it, he remains indifferent.

Good policies in relation to long-term governance of resources and preservation of biological species will lead to much better future for all subjects of the holistic model. Such policies will contribute immensely for the building of much more stable bonds between the different participants in a holistic organization.

How should be determined the legal interest of the subjects of the holistic model?

In order to be protected an interest of a subject in the first place the group entity should be thoroughly studied. The legal interest of humankind can be well defined by people, who have proved that they have a profound understanding of the human psyche, human rights and the conditions which are a prerequisite for development of humanity.

All aspects of its legal interest require in-depth research in relation to humane development of the civilization and protection of the rights of every human, without regards its citizenship. Because for humankind every human being is its unique manifestation, every person should have opportunities for an easier access to healthy goods and to the modern achievements of the society.

In relation to the interests of animals, plants and the Earth, it is logical to give priorities to the sound scientific conclusions of researchers who know the lives of these organisms and understand what is good for their development and which environment is beneficial for them.

Recognizing the importance of each individual and each collective as well as the provision of conditions for them to choose freely their path of development is of paramount importance to build harmonious bonds with them and to satisfy the interests of the whole.

If the trend is contrary to the established legal interests of the whole, the holistic organization applies holistic methods of influence. They differ significantly from the imposition of repressive sanctions, which is a characteristic of the egoistic systems. More details on the principles of humanistic correctional impact and the institute of humane restorative reaction are presented in chapter seven.

Ever subject of the holistic model has a legitimate legal interest which has to be recognized and to be a determining factor in making of management decisions. This means that the inability of most people to communicate with plants, animals and the Earth should not lead to the neglect of their interests, such as keeping them in poor conditions and leaving biological species and the planet die. Meeting the needs of all of them should be made anteriorly and in the best possible way for the specific time by applying a holistic approach. More details about the holistic approach are presented in chapter four.

When there is an opposition of the legitimate legal interests between subjects, which at the given moment cannot be simultaneously satisfied, the guiding principle is that with priority is the interest of the subject, which is higher in the hierarchy of the legal interests. When it is absolutely necessary to outstep the boundaries of a lower-standing subject and to violate its interest, this should be performed in the least possible way. An example of such a collision is the necessity of using plants as a food resource for animals and humans.

In the hierarchy of the legal interests those of human are logically placed as higher than those of animals and plants. The interests of plants, from its side should be perceived as such with a priority over those of plants.

Positioning the interests of Earth in the hierarchy requires reviewing our planet as a sole living being, which also is an individual manifestation of the Absolute and the whole. We should highlight that in case of an insuperable contradiction between the interests of the planet and to its biological inhabitants, which could lead to significant damage of Earth, or even to its destruction, a priority should be given to the interests of the planet over those of humankind, or the rest of the species. Building of a harmonious relationship between humankind and Earth mainly depends on the humans and therefore such collision can be avoided, if humankind cherishes the planet that is supporting it. Such protection of Earth can be successfully achieved through the application of a holistic economy.

All organizations of humans such as states, international organizations and private corporations should be viewed through the prism of whether they satisfy the interests of humankind and the whole. In order to describe the holistic model, it is necessary firstly to clarify the relations on a deeper level - those of biological species- humans, animals, plants and Earth as a planet which is supporting their life.

Every social system has a purpose for which it has been created, even if it is not clearly defined in society. The purpose of the capitalistic system is to serve the ruling elite by producing more and more goods. Because of that, the interests of the subjects of the holistic model are not leading for this type of egoistic system. The methods to achieve control over humanity are related to managing the access to resources, which are needed for survival and for all kind of projects.

Through regulation of access to goods, the humans are forced to perform an assigned job, in order to survive and keep themselves in their social class and climbing to a higher one. This work force is used to satisfy the egoistic interest of the employer/assignor and not the interest of the whole. In the relatively open capitalistic societies the person is driven to move up in a higher socio-economic class. Pursuing this aim as an end itself can cause many social problems and its existence leads to moral and spiritual degradation of the person and of all humankind. The reason is that the attention of society is largely removed from what we are doing for the outer world to what we are receiving from it in the form of power over others, money and access to goods.

One of the main shortcomings of the capitalistic system is that in order to be manageable, it should convince all parties that there is a shortage of resources. If such doesn't exist, the resource is gradually taken under control, financially evaluated and sold, so that it can be presented as limited and unavailable to all. This leads to an artificial deformation of the environment and inhuman indifference to the participants in the system, because everything in this system is perceived as a means of service to the ego.

CHAPTER 3

CHARACTERISTICS OF THE HOLISTIC MODEL

*„ He stood at the foot of the Stairs - a high white staircase
of rose-flecked marble."*

„The tale of the stairs", Hristo Smirnenski

Among the main characteristics of every social model, beside the aim for its creation, are the governing methods that are used and the ways to motivate the participants.

The capitalistic model and partially the communistic one are those that are dominating worldwide and continue to be imposed over societies until present day. Before we analyze what are the characteristics of the holistic model, it is useful to trace what kind of worldview, relations and values have offered us both existing systems.

The ideal capitalistic model delaminates society in such a way that large groups of people (between 3-12 %), who are significant parts of a well-developed capitalistic state, are placed below the class of the working poor.[11] These are people who often cannot find a job; do not have a home and enough income to cover their basic needs. In the academic researches for social stratification, they are defined as "underclass" people.[12] It is logical to ask the question: why it is necessary for the capitalistic system to place so many people at the bottom of society? Why it is unable to stimulate their development, inclusion and encouraging them being responsible towards themselves and society? Why are not implemented the normal humane governing activities which can prevent the individual to achieve the social bottom? Could these people deliberately been left in the lurch to fulfill a particular social role which the capitalist system needs? If it is so, what is the significance of this role?

---

11 Gilbert, D. *The American Class Structure: In An Age of Growing Inequality*, Belmont, CA: Wadsworth, 2002
12 Ibid.

In order to reply honestly to these questions, it is necessary to remember how man is changing, led by the driving force of self-service and what is pushing him to move forward? This is the fear for survival, which turns into greed and striving for domination.

In all capitalistic societies this stratum of "underclass" people has a clearly defined purpose and social role. They are an example for the representatives of the working poor and the working class what will happen, if they quit their job, or refuse to obey their employer. In this way fear is used again as a primary motivator for everyone to look for a job and to get on the wheel of the working process, without being very attentive to the needs of people, planet, plants or animals. Because of this fear, people cannot be very mindful and fastidious about the conditions of the jobs on the free market. It is not desired from them to evaluate the global impact of a profession and of the system in general.

This logic continues up on the ladder: the workers are negative example for the lower middle class, which is itself a negative example for the upper middle class and so on. These segregated relations between the different classes lead to neglect of the interests of humankind, which is expressed mainly in the respectful and equal humane treatment of every human, as a manifestation of humankind and the Absolute.

The circumstance that every lower class serves as an example for the fall of a participant from a higher class often stimulates arrogance and hostility among members of different socio-economic classes. The capitalistic model maintains firmly the attitudes of inhumane indifference, exploitation and disrespectful treatment of others. These qualities deform human nature and build the twisted concept that someone is more important than another, because he is located in an upper socio-economic class in the capitalistic system. Capitalism is capable to evaluate the net worth of a person to the cent which completely devalues his spiritual origin and purpose of existence.

These attitudes become the most robust prison for the human, because they are deluding him to perceive capitalist social stratification as something natural which is valuable and worth preserving.

The so called "underclass" participants in a capitalistic state have one more important purpose. Many of these people are causing social disturbance and committing crimes. They are easily susceptible to external influences and different forms of addiction. They are one of the most important clients of social and other services in the capitalistic state. Law enforcement departments are receiving additional funding to try to protect the other citizens from this class. Healthcare system can function at full speed just to try to treat one of their many health problems. Social services, judicial system, insurers, arms manufacturers and many other subsystems and economic branches are justifying their existence, because the capitalistic social stratification foresees this step on the ladder. The weakest and most vulnerable participants in the capitalistic state will shuffle off there. Those, who will be able to change their social status, will leave a free place for another person, which means that the model will continue to function intact. This purpose of the underclass step in the ladder shows the distorted face of capitalism and the desire of this system to maintain certain problems and not to resolve them comprehensively.

Here it is important to clarify that not all people are fully succumbed into these ethically fallen attitudes, but the mere existence of a social model which is maintaining them makes humanistic and ecologic values hardly asserted causes for an individual or a small group of people.

Because the separate person is focused not to prolapse of the class that he is, or strives to move in a higher one, he is interested less and less what is happening in the overall environment and for what purpose is used his added value, which he has produced with his labor. Capitalism is not stimulating people to be interested in how is used and applied the result from their labor and whether the products they have created are beneficial for the whole. It is so, because egoistic systems do not intend to satisfy in the best way the needs of their participants and to serve as a bridge for better relations. Instead these systems are considering humans as biological robots which are supposed to produce more and more quantum. This conclusion defines capitalistic system as a prison with the main objective to control and subdue humanity.

Capitalism focuses the attention of a human being to protect his own micro-world, which consists primarily of family and closest people. Every risk and every threat for this tiny personal reality is purposefully maintained by the system, in order to prevent the person to further expand his consciousness for more comprehensive forms of community and not to be able to feel and live the unity with the whole humankind and the whole world.

The communistic model emerges as an ideological antipode of the problems, caused by capitalism, among which is the child labor, violation of women's rights, exploitation of the working class, low income for most of the society which is jeopardizing their access to goods and services and overall dehumanization of society.

These problems continue to be topical and the personal opinion of the author is that the proposed communistic model and the ways of its enforcement could not achieve the goals that they were called upon and caused even worse violations of rights. Among them is the disregard of the free will of the person, dictatorship, forceful deprivation of private property, killing and imprisoning those who think differently and are critical, political persecutions and repressions. The removal of free entrepreneurship and free public discussions of ideas about what is in the interest of society and what is not presents another form of repression, which is a characteristic not only for the implementation, but also for the theory of building communistic system.

The holistic model is a fundamentally different model than the capitalistic and the communistic and it does not share the principles of changing the social system by force and imposing ideology and beliefs to the people. Every political ideology, which professes that maxim "the end justifies the means" is doomed to violate the humane ideals, which it claims to pursue (if there are such ideals at all). Each and every action should be an expression of these ideals, consequently every means need to be in resonance with the end, which is set. The communistic model is imposed to society and turns the system into a rigid prison for individuals who do not want to be part of this system and who do not recognize its values and their way of implementation. This type of system is even more limitary than the capitalistic in the field of right and freedoms of people. It does not allow criticism neither to the ideology, nor its application.

Capitalistic and communistic models do not aim to build a harmonious society, which exploits only what is desirable for the planet to handle, or take into consideration the interests of humankind, animals and plants. This aim is firstly set in the holistic model of organizing society and it is the cornerstone of every organization and unit, build on the holistic principles.

The holistic system should become a network of many holistic organizations, which are syncing their policies and activities between each other. This system aims to facilitate and support those efforts of an individual or an organization, which would lead to overall improvements of the life of all subjects of the holistic model.

Nowadays, there isn't a state which applies fully capitalistic or communistic doctrines. In the capitalistic states there is some sort of social policy and efforts are made to control corporate greed, and in the communistic states, if we assume that such still exists, there is private property, economic stratification in classes, internal commerce between private subjects, competition in the economy.

Both systems are growing by stimulating fear for survival among people. However, communism is suppressing the free will of the individual and turning him into a voiceless executor of the state, while capitalism is trying to "widen the loop" and direct the thoughts of its participants to comply with the system for which it rewards them with goods and status.

Despite their flaws on a principle level, both types of egoistic systems have also positive sides, which have been taken into consideration and have been integrated in the holistic model. For example, in the last at the same time are guaranteed the freedoms of individuals to create and produce, but at the same time it is guided and stimulated to be in the service to the whole, without the state (or private organization) to abdicate from protecting the economic rights of the people. These economic rights are not understood as an abstract possibility to buy and sell something, but as **the real right to receive public goods for free equally with the other participants**. The holistic model is constructed with the understanding that every human being has to have the opportunity to choose what beneficial deeds he wants to do for others, to have the right to be qualified for that particular area and to be always free to choose whether to participate in a specific project or not. For the holistic governance is of crucial importance what is the product of a private organization or a state, how this product is made, to whom it is available and for what purposes it will be used for.

The new model differs significantly from the capitalism and in terms of attitudes that stimulate people to interact with other living organisms and the environment. The leading capitalistic attitude is exploiting everyone, including Earth, animals and plants, while the holistic model focuses on the responsibility that humankind has for the harmonious development of other species and the planet.

The main characteristics of the holistic model, which has to be applied in the process of creating a holistic organization, are the following:

1. The holistic model is **altruistic**. This means that **society stimulates the creation of goods for the benefit of the whole, with the aim to meet the needs of all participants in the system**. This model differs from the capitalistic, which is based on the desire for profit at the expense of others.

According to Miriam Webster dictionary the definition of the word altruism is: "*feelings and behavior that show a desire to help other people and a lack of selfishness*". This definition illustrates some of the features through which we can understand whether a person is led by altruism, or egoism, but it cannot show us why a person is willing to do different beneficial things to others and why he maintains this attitude.

The participants in the holistic system are aware to some extent that they are one with others and are joyful, satisfied and with a sense of purpose, when they can be beneficial and of service to them. Being aware of the oneness means also that the suffering of others is felt like yours. This is an additional motivation of the person to be compassionate and to help those in need.

Altruism is a philosophy in which a person or other being understands himself as something more than just his ego and his thoughts and actions are directed towards selfless service to other being in a right way, in the right time and with the right means.

Altruism is not a waste of energy, or creating dependence with an individual which is jeopardizing his development. Contrary to popular belief, the altruistic attitude doesn't always lead to deprivation to those, who is exercising it. In the cases, when someone altruistically is giving something to another person, this form of sacrifice should be timely, accurate and necessary for the harmonious development of the person who is receiving it, but ultimately for both the receiver and the giver. The altruistic attitude is equal to feeling love towards another being. It is a knowing of union with another human being, other living organism, or a collective. Therefore, it is fair not to limit the scope of altruism only to people, as it can include also other beings.

It would be wrong to refer as altruism only the act of giving of material goods to someone. It cannot be comprehensively defined with concrete actions, which can be characterized as supportive, because there can be different motives (including selfish) for the provision of a good.

There are a variety of examples of such motives, which are different than altruistic ones. Among them are:

1) Targeted investment - giving something, which in the future will give a return in a material or other form for the giver;

2) Luring - giving away with the intention to be created favorable attitude towards the giver, so that it can be exploited with selfish purposes in the future;

3) Exploitation of dependence - the gift is provided in order to be created a bond of dependence between the giver and the receiver;

4) Creation of dependence - the gift is provided in order to be created a bond of dependence between the giver and the gift;

5) Purposeful provision of an item which the receiver cannot is not prepared to use in a way, which can lead to its harmonious development;

6) Provision of good with the false expectation that the receiver will not abuse it. In order to avoid that, altruistic attitude requires in-depth knowledge of both the person and the gift;

7) Provision of a gift for which can be assumed that it cannot be protected by the receiver. Typical example of such cases is proliferation of knowledge and materials for nuclear weapons or other knowledge to states and organizations which are not sufficiently capable to protect it. In the altruistic attitude is necessary to be embedded responsibility, which includes knowledge of the environment in which

the potential receiver is functioning, his attitude towards the good and his capability to protect it, if he receives it. Therefore, it is important the giver not to be naïve, but well-informed about the expected outcome of the situation, if the good is provided;

8) Ostensibly altruistic behavior, which aims to create trust, which can be further exploited for selfish purposes.

Many other examples can be given for a behavior which resembles a result from altruistic attitude, but in reality it serves selfish intentions.

Altruism does not necessarily mean to give something to someone, without receiving something in return. For example, one person may sell a good to a customer, but with the clear intention and main motive the receiver to have specific benefit from it and improve his life. The criterion in this case is which motivation stands higher - the profit or the benefit of the customer. Capitalistic societies does not consider such intentions, but they can be traced in extraordinary situations when the profit can be left aside in order not prevent the positive impact of a good or service. In the normal transactions and business activities the received money are a necessary means for the seller to perform his activities and provide his goods or services, because he probably lives in a capitalistic system.

The altruistic attitude doesn't necessarily include the provision of goods. It can be in the form of non-interference or actions, which are aimed to prevent the person to reach an object, which would lead to his disharmony and those of the whole.

We can draw the conclusion that the attitude to act in the interest of another being and to use proper behavior in the process of applying this attitude, are the features of altruism. They should be applied between the subjects of the holistic model in order to create a system of service to the whole. The holistic model of social organizing is considered altruistic, because the aim of working process and of the holistic economy is to satisfy the interest of the whole and improving the life of the participants in the system. The leading motive to do a job is not to gain goods and building social status, as it is in the egoistic societies, but to improve the life of all. This aim requires much deeper planning of the actions and distribution of resources.

2. The holistic model requires all participants in the corresponding organization to treat each other as equally important individual manifestation of the Absolute and the whole. This viewpoint serves as a basis for the principle that the system should provide equal or approximately equal opportunities for development of the spiritual potentials (talents) of its participants. They are free to choose the field and the way to satisfy the interests of the whole. The creation of optimal conditions for development of everyone and the provision of equal access to goods, which are public property, are the two most important features, which distinguish the social aspects of the holistic model from the capitalistic and communistic ones. These features define it as **humanistic** and **harmonious**. In the holistic model there is no division of society in classes through a quantitative criterion of wealth, in order to determine to which social class a person belongs. This is a logical conclusion, considering the principle that participants have an equal access to goods from public property and they are supposed to be sufficient for the needs of everyone in the system. The relevant criteria for differentiation of the participants are the type of their activities, interests, participation in projects, imitativeness, and experience in finding solutions of problems. All these activities are synchronized and integrated to satisfy the interests of the whole and at the same time lead to forming the best possible conditions for personal development of everyone. On the basis of the mentioned criteria a person rises in the hierarchy of the organization in the service to the whole, without being treated as more important than others and without receiving additional access to goods as a form of reward. To import terminological clarity, it should be pointed that an organization, which is build, according to the principles of the holistic model is called **holistic organization**. The bond between a holistic organization and its participant is unique and develops the perception of indispensability of everyone, which is not typical for egoistic social systems. The holistic model is created in theory to restrict and prevent generic privileges, political appointments, lobbying influence, career development without preparation and other unprofessional forms of occupying positions, which are typical for the systems of service to self.

3. The participation in holistic organization is always **voluntary**. The free will of everyone to apply for inclusion and to leave is an important condition for its successful building and development. The right of the individual is to choose to be part of this community, to adopt its main ideals and principles and participate in their realization. If the person is an adult, who is mentally fit, he should have the right to choose whether to be part of such organization or not. The principle of voluntary inclusion is an absolute necessity for the holistic organization, because the methods for stimulation of the participants are not related so much to with coercion and deprivation of access to goods, which is typical for egoistic systems. This completely different approach towards governance would not be easily adopted by many people, who sincerely desire change, but who are not ready to release their egoistic attitudes.

The ideological advantage of the holistic system over all known egoistic systems is its aim to provide better and better care for all its participants, to respect their individuality and to treat them as equally important to the organization.

The freedom of the individual in a holistic organization extends also to the legal order of the organization. Legal norms, adopted in a holistic organization are not imposed over the participants. Instead, the basic principles are explained to everyone and they are free to accept them en bloc, if they want to be part of the holistic organization. This is a higher understanding of the meaning of the concept of "social contract".

Compliance with all legal norms of the organization is a personal choice, expressed by the individual in a declaration. This form of acceptance is an expression of the trust and commitment of the person to the fundaments of the community and from the way of his adherence to it, the community will build its trust towards the individual. In cases of doubt in the rightness and necessity of a certain norm, every participant has the right to receive an official explanation of its meaning and purpose. This is an important part of the social contract and the dialogue on improving the way the society functions. Every person has a subjective perception and worldview and he deserves the chance to receive a proper explanation of the principles and norms of the holistic organization.

The right of the participant to receive an explanation of the norm is followed by another of set of rights - to express his view on the norm; to make argumentative proposals for changes; to receive substantiated official replies on his proposal. This form of dialogue and individual bond between the person and the organization on the fundamental principles and purpose of specific norms is not typical for the present day societies, because the subjects in a state are supposed to obey the norms and follow the rule of law. Contrariwise, the holistic approach towards governance considers the freedom of the individual to declare observation of norms, as an absolute necessity and an imminent part of the social contract for the following reasons:

Firstly, it is a prerequisite of the right of everyone to choose the principles and norms that will be guiding for him. The responsibility of a person for his own actions can be borne only if he is aware of the norms and if he has declared that is accepting them as guiding for his life in order to satisfy the interest of the whole. Without such declaration, it is not justified for the community to expect certain behavior from anyone. If a declaration is made by the participant, the breaching of norms in society would be a violation of his own intentions and not the will of the organization, which is imposed on him. In this situation the reaction of the organ which is responsible for protecting the norms in society have to be qualitatively different. The reason is that the holistic organization is trying to support the person in his choice of observing a concrete norm or principle. Instead of enforcing a punishment or other form of sanction, it has to use the institute of humane restorative reaction. More information on the purpose and features of this institute are presented in chapter seven.

If a holistic organization is governed poorly and some of its members do not want to contribute for its development, or reconsider their participation in it, they can leave at any time with all of their private property. This is a sure guarantee that the community will retain its purpose to function in the interest of the whole and at the same time will respect others who do not share this view anymore. The logic of implementation of these measures is to avoid repressive punishment of people and understand the deeper reasons for crimes and unlawful behavior. Humane restorative reaction serves as an instrument which supports the person in the permanent process of integration of different interests and values.

Secondly, the holistic organization takes into consideration that every person has an individual worldview and unique filters of perception and therefore it is necessary to exist an opportunity for him to receive a proper explanation of the legal norms. This explanation includes a comparison with other legal norms and the rationale why they are serving the interest of the whole. The legal order of modern day societies doesn't take into consideration whether a person understands the rule of a legal norm and the system does not provide any resources for explanation and clarification on individual basis to every person. The reason is that the law in these systems is an imposition of the external will of the state over the person. There is no doubt whatsoever that this is an imposition, because the will of the person is not regarded and also because the legal norm is encapsulated with sanctions, if the person doesn't obey the rule. The holistic system, on the other hand, relies on the responsibility of the person to fulfill his own promise, in the form of declaration of acceptance the norms, that he will follow the rules, which are incorporated in them. The threat and the repressive punishment are unacceptable forms of oppression, deprivation of freedom to choose your own behavior and methods which are causing human rights violation. They are a feature of societies which are not free. The holistic society develops its legal order, observing simple logic: A person should be acquainted with a norm of the society, then he should express his will whether he accepts the rule or not to be guiding in his life and only then the society may have expectations from this person what would be his behavior.

The third reason, why such a dialog between the individual and the organization is needed is related to the developing of the system. Thanks to such dialog a unique perspective could be expressed and unique solutions could be proposed. The freedom of everyone to make grounded proposals for amendments of legislation, which are also argumentatively accepted or rejected, following strict criteria, is a guarantee for improving society and its legal order. The right of every individual to make proposals for changes of the system is an expression of his freedom to participate in a holistic society and an indication of the willingness of the society to improve itself and further develop on the path of service to the whole.

The process of lawmaking through a direct dialogue and not only via representatives will be an affirmation of the freedom of people to contribute and to develop society. It substitutes the obligation to obey with the right to join. Such a right is a strong safeguard that people will exercise their freedom in a way which does not violate the contemporary norms and more importantly is aimed at better satisfaction of the interest of the whole. These are fundamental differences between holistic and egoistic systems. The last are applying sanctions in the form of destructive actions in order to subdue its subjects. In contemporary systems it is irrelevant whether a person accepts legal norms or not and this automatically violates his freedom and makes him a subservient subject, instead of a contracting one.

The democratic elections of members of parliament and other official representatives in a parliamentary state does not change the subservience of the person, because his will of acceptance or rejection of legal norms remains irrelevant for the state.

In the present day legal systems are not incorporated working mechanisms, which can turn argumentative proposals from any member of the society, into new legal norms. It is a common practice that collective demands for changes to have greater weight and to be considered with respect in the service to self systems, instead of the individual proposals. This is another indication that a guiding principle in these societies is the number of people behind a proposal and not the quality of the proposal itself.

Pathetically proclaimed principle of "Rule of law" is reduced to the blind acceptance of the will of the state over the personal will and the refusal of the individual to think and to choose whether to accept the legal norm or not. This limitation destroys the trust between the individual and the system. This principle jeopardizes the personal growth, because it bans the right of him to choose his way of life and to coordinate his behavior with others.

From the opposite side of this paradigm for society as a prison, the holistic organization is taking into regard the understanding that the development of an individual can be accomplished only if he exercises his free will in a frame, which he is not violating the right of others to exercise it and respects the interest of the whole. The functioning of the system in a way, which does not violate the rights of others and the whole, is closely related with prevention of destructive behavior, which hinders the harmonious developing of the potentials of the victim, of the perpetrator and of the whole community. Modern societies are adopting legal systems which are built on the motto "*If you do this, I will sanction you with this*". The holistic legal system builds a community on a motto in the form of a question: "*In order all of us to live better, will you respect the rights of others and avoid their violation*? This type of lawmaking requires assent on behalf of the person in the organization. The necessity of such assent displays the next characteristic of the holistic model - **contractual origin.**

4. The principle of contractual origin is simultaneously a validation of the freedom of the individual to choose whether to participate in a community or not, and guarantee the freedom of the community to accept the individual as well. This form of agreement is useful for both sides, because it clarifies what attitude and behavior they could expect from each other. Besides freedom, contractual negotiation is also equality between the individual and the community. The contract is the ground for both sides to demand from each other certain behavior. In it are included the rights and duties, which they agree to have between each other. The contractual origin is also a manifestation of the consensual acceptance of a particular person in the organization and his statement of respect of the ideals, values and rules of the community.

The holistic model requires that the concordance of will of the participant and the holistic organization to be concluded in conformity with the interest of the whole. In practice, this agreement is a comprehensive employment contract, which consists of many rights and obligations between both parties. Choosing and if necessary creating a satisfactory working position for both parties, with activities which are beneficial for the whole, including the employee, is the core feature of the contract. Part of this agreement is also the basic norms, which are in force in the organization. If there is a mutual consent between both parties this contractual relationship can be changed in the part of due behavior of the participant, especially when the interests of the whole would be better protected. Such changes cannot affect in a negative way the rights of the person. An example of such change is the type of practices profession. Parameters of the treaty, which regulate the equality of the person with all other participants, cannot be changed, because this will violate the basic principle of the holistic organization of equal access to public goods. Privileges of participants cannot be granted and rights cannot be violated, in order to prevent class differentiation of groups, based on economic grounds, which is typical for service to self systems. This means that the management personnel would not receive bigger access to public goods, or other egoistic economic stimulus, than the rest of the participants. Freedom in contemporary societies does not include negotiation between citizens and state whether law should be obeyed, or which norms should be improved. The acquaintance of the person with the legal norms is not even a prerequisite for a required behavior. The so called "social contract" does not include any form of individual consent of the rules of the community. Presently, the dissent with a particular legal norm that a person might have would not provide him with the right to substantiate an improved norm, which serves better the interest of the community and would not lead to change of the legal order, because of this proposal. For example, if a person doesn't want a death penalty to be applied in his own state, it is irrelevant what arguments he adduces of the barbarity, inhumanity and incorrigibility of this sanction and it will remain. The holistic organization relies on its participants to be developed and improved. Therefore, it considers the arguments of their proposals and if they would lead to better satisfaction of the interests of the whole, the organization is obliged to implement them.

5. The next main characteristic of the holistic model is its **transparency**, which is in much greater extent than in capitalistic societies. It includes the right of every participant to know for what purpose will be used the result of his labor and what are the aims of a specific project in which he is working. The provision of this information is a key element in fulfilling the promise of a free society in service to the whole. It is because the person will choose to participate in a working process, which he is drawn into and he will bear responsibility for the proper implementation of his tasks. People, who are aware of the overall positive effects of their deed and the project itself, are much more involved in the process and mindful of the results, because they are feeling part of something much bigger than themselves and something that makes a difference. The right

of information of every participant in the holistic organizations for what purposes would be used his labor force should be guaranteed, because it would determine to large extent the reason for volunteering in a project or not being directly involved in it. The exercise of an informed choice from every participant is a prerequisite for their personal growth, maturity and an additional stimulus for achieving good governance of the holistic organization. The transparency of the multilayered positive effect of the project and the results of specific actions are a strong impulse for completing the work with inspiration and not through coercion with threats of sanctions and poverty, as is the practice of egoistic systems.

Transparency is an expression of the right of the participants to be informed and to monitor the development of the organization and choosing in which aspect to be involved. Transparency is a natural continuation of the freedom of the individual to be part of the holistic society. In the systems of service to self the labor of the employee is used as the employer desires. It is very often that people are not aware for what purpose will be used the software they are writing, the scientific research that they are doing and even the building that they are constructing.

Capitalism does not require from corporations to develop society and it is not justified and logical to place such an expectation over a private subject, because its main aim is to survive in a competitive environment of the system. Therefore, genius discoveries of brilliant scientists would not be introduced for massive application in modern society, because this would lead to a larger freedom, which a corporation or a state doesn't desire at that particular moment. A typical example is scientific discoveries for use of a renewable source of energy and their slow and limited introduction in the economy, because the effect of it is undesirable for leading energy companies and leading states.

In a holistic organization the scientific discoveries are applied in service to the whole and the development of all economic sectors is not bound with a mandatory profit. These principles are main advantage over the egoistic systems in which an economic product is made in order to lead to certain dependence of the customers and to bring profits.

Transparency of the holistic system is an additional guarantee that politics, economy and science would be implemented in benefit of humankind and in the interest of the whole.

6. The holistic model is **open** for a career development of all participants in the system and encourages empowering of a person with additional responsibilities in correspondence with his expertise, ethics and experience, so that the interest of the whole is protected. The system should be able to adopt itself, if the person desires to change his activities. Such changes do not lead to increase or decrease of his income, property status and access to public goods and services. One of the most important features of the holistic society and a dividing red line with the values of the egoistic states and corporations is the principle that material goods are not used as a reward and a stimulus for a particular behavior in a community. The acquisition of commodities and services which are public property is a right of every participant, which has to be fulfilled. Equal access to public goods is a key principle for satisfaction of these rights and to be implemented in practice the declared principle of economic equality of all participants. For the execution of activities every person will need a specific access to goods, depending on his position. This access should not be considered as a reward of the person, or as egoistic stimulus for the occupation of a particular position. For example, if activities in outer space are needed to be performed, the astronaut will need access to the space craft, proper technical equipment and training. All these resources are needed for the normal provision of the space activities and it is not a form of reward. The logical conclusion is that the goods, which are needed for the performance of a specific activity in the holistic organization, are not in the scope of public goods, which have to be distributed with equal access to all participants. For egoistic societies is typical the intentional misuse of the criteria which goods are functionally needed for a specific activity and which are luxury and an act of lavishing public resources. Egoistic civilizations provide for every class of people different goods and services in matter of quality. They are also limited. This inequality in the access to goods in capitalistic society generates deep sense of identity of the person to his ego and property, which is in fact determinative of his place in such society.

The openness of the holistic model requires avoiding every form of discrimination in relation to career development in the organization.

As was mentioned above, the criteria whether a participant would take more responsibilities in the holistic organization are his expertise, ethics and experience. At first glance they may seem the same with the presently existing rules in modern states, but this is not true. In democratic societies the criterion for obtaining political power is the number of people, who are supporting a particular party or a person, and not the impartial, thorough evaluation of management decisions, which are proposed by a person or by a group of people. Presently, it is considered normal practice those, who won the elections to distribute executive positions as rewards to trusted people and leaders of the winning party. The political appointments are presented as a natural process of a party to be responsible to the people. From a holistic point of view this form of distribution of governmental positions lead to bad management and bias towards private interests and not the interests of the whole. Big corporations are usually lobbying very aggressively and influencing the nomination of a person and the policy that he is supposed to execute, so that it is convenient for them. For example if a scientist in the field of medicine discovers a cure, which can be easily accessible, but medical corporations and state are willing to profit from the process of harnessing the symptoms of this disease, the cure would not be distributed freely to the people, who needs it.

The holistic system is not interested in making profit on the expense of the people, because its aim is their beneficial and harmonious development. In the example of the discovered cure all available resources should be directed towards making it freely available for all participants, who might need it. Since all goods and services, which are public property, are provided freely to the participants and are aimed in the interest of the whole, it is logical that medicaments are also free for everyone in the holistic organization.

In a holistic state the healthcare policy would be led by people, who are capable to organize the process of finding the best possible ways of prevention and cure of the population and not by people, who are capable of compliance and implementation of the lobbyist interests in the healthcare and of the process of making money from people's sickness. The openness of the holistic system provides much more opportunities for people, who are skillful in satisfaction of the interests of the whole, to be responsible for managing decisions.

7. The application of the holistic model by a private organization or a state is a process, which can be defined also as **adaptive**. This includes changes in relation to subjects; relationships between participants and ways of management. It doesn't mean that the holistic organization will change the aim of its existence and the principles of freedom and equality of its participants. Adaptiveness is applicable only in the ways of implementing these principles, when a better satisfaction of the interests of the whole is possible. For example, when new participants are included in the community, their rights and legitimate interests have to be satisfied in the same way as those of the other participants. In the example of the loving family, in which a child is borne, it will receive attention and care from all members of the family. For the newborn will be distributed resources for its nurture. Ideally, a separate room will be furnished, or at least a corner of the room will be adapted. All available conditions will be provided for the normal and healthy upbringing of the child to the extent which is possible for the family. These changes affect all members of the family, who have to adjust and contribute, but they are needed for the natural equal and harmonious development of the whole community. In the same way the holistic system should be able to integrate its new members in the best possible way, focusing on the least possible mandatory adjustment of the other participants and maintaining equal access to public goods for all members. New participants can be newborn children, but also newly accepted members, who are concluding an agreement with the organization.

In the inevitable cases of discovering new biological species, they should be regarded as part of the whole and therefore treated with respect, observing their rights and taking into consideration their interests. Newly discovered species should be studied and protected. For this purposes public resources should be allocated for its normal life in an environment in which these species are improving their relationships with others. When it is possible, the self-awareness of living beings should be developed in direction that they understand themselves as manifestation of the Absolute and part of the whole.

Another form of adaptation of the holistic organization is related with the possibility of improving the relationships between participants, so that the interest of the whole is better protected. This may be the introduction of a new scientific knowledge or finding a better way of organizing the community. All newly gained knowledge, which widens the understanding of the subjects of the holistic model, should be considered and applied by the holistic organization. This will lead to permanent optimization and constant improving of the relationships between the participants in the organization, in order to develop the holistic society. The holistic organization encourages the scientific progress in the service to the whole and all results which can be applied as goods and services should be made freely available to all members. The development of the social relationships is conducted by the provision of opportunity to renegotiate the contract between a participant and the holistic organization. An important principle in the process of renegotiation is that the rights of every participant, including access to goods, cannot be limited without their consent. In order to be developed the social relations in the holistic society, the rights of the participants should be increased, their scope widen and this should be made simultaneously for everyone. Therefore, the acceptance of new participants in the organization should not lead to decrease of access to goods and limitation of the rights for older participants. If it is absolutely necessary, this cannot be conducted without the explicit consent of those, who are affected.

8. Another important feature of the holistic model is the relevance of **argumentation** in the decision-making process. This feature implies that the organization is developed according to grounded proposals and solid argumentation in every decision-making, which can be analyzed and evaluated by an existing algorithm and methodology. This is another distinctive "red line" feature between holistic and egoistic systems. In the last, the criteria of social development and the directions are unclear in the same way as is unclear the distinction of private and public interest.

Modern day institutions are not legally obliged to motivate their decisions and to clarify why the proposed decision is the best one in the present moment. Control of official misconduct and abuse of power are related with another institution and not with the quality of the act. In the judicial system we can trace this in the institutionalization of the judicial instance as a form of guarantee of good judiciary.

In the legislature legal acts are adopted with majority and not necessarily because of the logic of the arguments of the proposal. The executive authority is not obliged to present the arguments, which justify the decisions and show clearly why they are optimal for the specific time frame.

The holistic model is not aimed at institutionalism in general, as every organization is capable to function through its organs and institutions. However, the holistic organizations will use mechanisms, which shall guarantee in much larger extent that in all institutions are appointed the most capable people, who understand the interest of the whole in depth. Such mechanisms are not well developed in egoistic societies and proves of this statement are around us - in the form of representatives of political elite from all over the world.

In the holistic organization every decision, adopted by a particular organ, should be well grounded and have to show how the interest of the whole would be better protected, because of it.

The evaluation of the arguments shall be performed, following clearly defined criteria and algorithm, which will be researched in future publications. In this way the governance of the organization, its scientific and technological development shall be aimed in directions, which are in the interest of the humankind, animals, plants and the Earth.

Taking into account whether a decision corresponds to the interest of the humankind is missing in the service to self systems. It is enough to point out that states are still waging war campaigns, which means to send humans to kill other humans in the name of territorial disputes and selfish geo-political ambitions.

The holistic society places humankind above every national interest and stands on the principle that war is an absolutely last resort of means to dissolve international disputes, applicable only when it prevents drastic violation of the interest of the whole.

Every organization is created in the frame of a specific structure, which includes organs and relationships between them. For the different types exist similar organograms, which set to a large extent the interaction between participants in the organization. The structure itself is very important, because it indirectly affects the paths of developments of the community. Every state has its unique characteristics of governmental structure and institutions, but it is visible that there are considerable similarities in state's models. Corporations in all states also have similarities in their structures, organs and functions. They are legally regulated and because of that changing of their organizational model would be really difficult to happen. On a personal level, families also are shaped by specific models. In some cultures they include polygamy, in others same-sex marriages and so on.

Main characteristic of the holistic model is that it is basic for all other organizational models in a community, which desires to function in the service to the whole. It is a primary model, which serves as a landmark for the creation of all organizations and because of that its characteristics are transferred in all of them. The holistic model can be present in communities, including families, private organizations, states and humankind, who are willing to organize themselves in service to the whole.

The common elements of application of the holistic model in every organization are rooted in building a dignified attitude towards all participants and regarding them as unique manifestations of the Absolute and part of the whole. The holistic community is formed in such a way that its development can contribute to the interests of the whole in the best possible way in a respective moment.

CHAPTER 4

HOLISTIC APPROACH

"Divide and rule", the politician cries;
"Unite and lead", is watchword of the wise

Johann Wolfgang von Goethe

The systems in the service to self are using the approach "divide and conquer" in order to rule their members. In their mind is placed the thought of survival and in their hearts the fear of not being able to live well and be appreciated by society. This combination serves as a tool to guarantee obedience. Greed becomes the leading attitude and it stimulates economic growth in a competitive and tensed environment.

The holistic model and the organizations in the service to the whole, created on its pattern, use entirely different approach to build unity among the participants and reaching abundance for everyone. A distinctive feature of this approach is that it aims to build lasting and harmonious relationships of cooperation in the system and an attitude of considering everyone as a biological cell of a larger organism in which there is no competition. At the same time we have to repeat again that every participant is treated as a unique manifestation of the Absolute, a living cosmos, who has to be protected and supported by the holistic organization to develop freely.

Fear for the survival is unwanted condition, because it will obscure the bond of the individual with the whole, it will block joy and creativity and it will make the lower selfish attitude to be the leading one in his life. In order to prevent this downgrade, the holistic model uses approach and governance, which provide a safe and pleasant environment, which has to serve as a basis for free and creative development of the society in the path of service to the whole.

Through the provision of equal access to public goods, the individual is stimulated to be aware of himself as an important part of the holistic community and he is motivated to work with a desire for its development. In this way goods shall not be regarded by the participants as a primary aim of their work and main purpose of their life, as it is in the egoistic models of social governance.

The next feature of the holistic approach is that every project and every action are going through multilayered evaluation and is reviewed what is their influence in the whole environment is all areas.

The holistic approach is universal and it can be applied in all forms of social relations and in all areas of life. Its use can be on a micro level - in communicating with our friends, family, colleagues and in the internal structuring of a private organization, but it can be also on a macro level - in areas like state governance, global economy and labor process, policies, religion, science, education, social activities, health-care, ecology, internal affairs, international relations, etc.

Main characteristic of this approach is that the effect of every action has to be reviewed and evaluated simultaneously locally and globally. This will lead to constant improvement in the protection of the interests of the subjects of the holistic model and the whole itself.

This intention to satisfy the interests of the whole through all activities of every participant is the main difference with the aims, methods and approaches in the egoistic systems. In the last it is typical to be made many compromises with the interests of the poorly represented participants, as well as total ignorance of the interests of animals, plants and Earth at the expense of their economic exploitation.

In the process of applying the holistic approach, it is considered that all actions influence the whole system and all social relations in it. In order one action to be regarded as positive for the development of the holistic society its result should lead to better satisfaction of the interests of the participants and the whole, than before it was initiated.

The holistic approach foresees the improvements of a specific micro environment to result in improvements in the macro environment and the opposite - the developing of a macro environment should lead to better functioning on a micro level. Then we see protection of the interest of the whole.

For example a scientific institute (micro environment) perfects a technology for manufacturing of solar panels of thin foil, covered with nanoparticles. The application of this scientific discovery may satisfy to a larger extent the energy needs of the population of a state (macro environment), which leads to introduction of the technology to all separate energy consumers (another micro environment). Evaluating the positive effect of its activities, the state stimulates the best possible sustainability of the institute and encourages additional scientific work.

In the capitalistic economy estimations are made which suppliers of energy would lose money from a massive introduction of such scientific discovery; how to profit more from the technology and reduce the costs and quality in the process of its creation; what is the limited number of consumers of electricity, who would be its beneficial buyers; who is going to invest and search profit from this project.

A distinctive feature of the holistic approach is that decisions are made on the basis of scientifically grounded criteria and lobbying of private interests is not allowed. It is a well-known fact that lobbying is an unstoppable process in the capitalistic egoistic society and it is presented as a necessary part of decision-making. However, for the holistic society it is absolutely mandatory every activity to be planned carefully, so that it can satisfy many interests of the subjects. Every action should be evaluated as contributing to the protection of the interest of the whole, before it is initiated.

The holistic approach includes observing every system as a part of a bigger one, which in turn is part of even bigger one, etc. The bonds between these different in scale social organisms should be improved until they are working in unison as one organism, which is perpetual.

The holistic approach encourages an attitude of self-respect and honoring of others. This is achieved by building relationships, which are mutually beneficial for the participants and their environment.

The holistic approach includes management and working process which helps everyone to develop in a chosen direction. Participants are going to increase their knowledge and unwind their potentials in the most creative, satisfactory and joyful way, the organization is capable to provide. Therefore, survival struggle and competition are barriers in satisfying the interest of the whole and catalysts for destructive relationships between participants in a system. Instead, in the holistic society is applied a thorough cooperation on all level for satisfying separate individual and group interests in a balanced way.

In order a decision to be taken on a specific subject, it is always necessary to compare the proposals and to analyze the options for potential outcome. Such comparison is made by every person, starting from the smallest daily tasks and going to the vitally important decisions. The same assessment is conducted by all organizations in the process of decision-making. It has to be distinguished from the competition and the fight for dominance, which is typical for egoistic social systems. The competitors are willing to survive at all cost and they are interested to be chosen, without regards whether they provide a better solution or a useful product. This difference is very important, because competitors are willing to change the environment in their own interest, which is in conflict with the interest of the whole. They are inclined to thwart their competitor to win the race and even to participate in it; they lobby for themselves in front of those, who are making the decisions; they influence in every possible way, in order to be chosen to provide a specific service. These actions are performed from parties to electors, from corporations to consumers, from religious organizations to the laity. The result is service, which is expedient for the provider and not necessarily to the final beneficiary. This leads to a sequence of systematic problems in the egoistic systems, which shall not be created in the holistic society.

An important characteristic of the holistic approach is that all resources are aimed to satisfy the interest of the whole, while taking all proposals from the participants, applying the algorithm for decision making and informing them not only how they will be allocated, but also why certain activities are performed.

Clarification of the principles of allocation of resources on specific criteria is an absolute necessary prerequisite for good management of a holistic organization. This transparency would lead to finding even better options for satisfying the interest of the whole for the following reasons:

1. The participants in the system have the right to know the criteria and the argumentation behind every decision for distribution of goods and the direction of resources in a specific direction. The participants are part of the whole and they would be affected by those decisions to some extent. They may be consumers, if a good is made or users, if a service is provided. At the same time, they would be affected in one

way, if the holistic organization decides to invest in technical equipment for submerging scientific capsules in the ocean, and completely different field of knowledge will be stimulated if resources are allocated for space satellites and rockets.

Transparency in information is a guarantee for good governance and monitoring from one hand, but it is also a form of additional stimulus for the participants to do a job. For example, if a worker is participating in the construction of a building in order to have a job for taking care of himself and his family, he would not be particularly stimulated to be interested in the purpose of this building. In this case he will not be sympathetic to the future activity that would take place in the building. He may be constructing a factory for vegetables and fruits, but also a concentration camp and the potential effect over his psyche, caused by both projects is completely different. If we consider the holistic approach, the worker will be calm and relaxed that he and his family is economically secured by the holistic organization, that he would not work for more than six hours a day and that he would have time for his family and friends and for himself. The worker would be informed in advance what construction projects would take place for realization and he is given the freedom to choose in which one he will participate. He may choose the construction site, that is closer to his home, or has the best entertainments in the neighborhood, but he can also apply much deeper motivation for work. This person would have the opportunity to assess how he can serve the interests of the whole through this project and how to make an impact in the world as a worker. There is a significant difference for the development of this person in application of the two different approaches. The freedom to choose to participate, the right to receive detailed information, which can be used to make the choice more aware, would involve most of the workers to a much larger extent in the construction of a building, instead of working for the daily wage and feeling close to the bottom class of a society.

The inability people to be used by a holistic organization for purposes that they are not willing to be part of due to ethical concerns is an important additional form of prevention against projects, which are destructive for the whole, as is the example of the concentration camp.

In a holistic organization all employees are participants, who receive a specific "field" of the social relations in order to be cultivated and guarded. Then they are able to place their attention to their work and to provide a constructive feedback about the challenges that they are facing. Every employee possesses a unique professional view over a specific area of work and he is the best possible person, capable to provide a feedback on a local level, because he would be directly involved.

Next, the worker would develop in a deeper level his bond with the whole system, which will elevate his personality in many other ways. He would be much more satisfied with his job and much more useful to himself and others in the remaining social roles and functions in his life. For this person it would be much less likely to commit a crime or other form of infringement against the interests of the whole, because he would feel himself as part of it. This form of deeper integration into the community would lead to positive development of his humane core self and it would stimulate manifestations of natural positive personal characteristics. Such a man would be less likely to be corrupt and demotivated. To be reached such an understanding, a complete change of the system is required and the holistic organization should make serious efforts for inclusion of all its participants.

2. The participants in the system who are directly involved in a project activity have the right to receive detailed information how and for what purpose would be used their labor and added value. They have the right to be part of the decision-making process on all subjects, relevant to the project. The right to participate in the decision-making process for those, who are involved in the project, would result in much higher level of commitment from them. Their professional development would be encouraged as well, because they would know that their expert opinion would be considered. Placing a focus on the professional governance, which is based on a wider gathering of information from every person, involved in the project, would guarantee proper satisfaction of the interest of the whole. This expert basis for governance means that decision-makers should be people with knowledge and experience in the concrete field, as well as people with integrity and capability to protect the interest of the whole.

The criteria for taking a higher position in a system of service to the whole are very different and often include qualities such as: capability of the person to comply with private party interests, corporate interests, as well as the determination to follow orders without asking questions and even when he is aware that the consequences will be devastating.

3. The right of being informed is complementary with the right to make proposals in a free society. All participants in a holistic organization have the right to make proposals for its improving and direction of development. The criteria which proposals would be approved are based on searching a better way to satisfy the interests of the whole by applying the holistic approach and by using a clear algorithm of evaluation. This form of comparison of ideas is not the competition, which is maintained in the present day capitalistic societies, because there is not a financial stimulus whatsoever for the participants and their economic status is never threatened and put on the table. The next essential difference is that the proposals which are improving the functioning of the organization and the system and for which there are enough resources would be realized. Therefore, the momentary lack of resources is not a stimulus for thinking of good ideas, as it is supposes to be in capitalistic societies. Lack of goods much more often hinders creativity than nourishing it. Provision of resources for every project in a system of service to the whole would be much easier than in the egoistic ones, because the goods and services are not going to be made progressively more expensive by every economic actor on the chain, as it is in capitalistic relations.

In long term holistic organizations would develop better and better capabilities to produce and to encourage people. This would result in possessing much more resources with very high quality, than all capitalistic states and corporations. Every approved project would eventually be implemented.

All states and corporations have chosen or were forced to pursue their vaguely formed interests on the basis of service to self in a conflict or competitive environment of existence. Because of their detachment from the interests of the whole, they are violating in large scale the interests of the subjects of the holistic model. This could be remedied by applying holistic approach and limiting egoistic attitude.

Holistic governance

What does it mean to govern a specific community?

On the surface level of analysis we can determine that governance includes the ability to understand the needs and formulate the interests of a governed community, the ability to set clear objectives and the will to organize the participants in such a way, so that they implement their appointed tasks.

When the chance for direct influence is missing, on a deeper level of analysis we can define governance as the ability of a subject to consciously influence a decentralized multi-layered environment through his behavior. Most often this happens through forming or partially setting the attitudes of the participants, because this will predetermine their actions and reactions. An example of such environment, where there is not a supreme authority of governance, but desired results are achieved by influencing the other subjects are international relations.

On a higher level of refinement of governance we should place the ability to set and remove boundaries between group subjects and relatively independent environments. The evaluation for a potential transformation of two subjects in the process of emerging or locking of their relations is crucial for this refined form of governance. The correct forecast of the results from such interaction and the ability for its initiation or blocking is a form of governance, which should be executed responsibly. In many cases these actions remain unknown for the affected subjects, who are only observing the effects of the newly opened opportunities, or the closing of the already existing ones. The subjects do not necessarily realize what the causes behind the changes they are witnessing are and what would be the consequences from their use. Even if they understand the causes and the effects, they are unable to regulate the specific processes. Examples of such an influence are: decisions for signing of a trade agreement; introduction of a new technology in the economy; presenting of a correct in-depth analysis of a specific historical event.

In the systems of service to the self, the guiding factor for the participants is the survival of the fittest. At some point they start to adapt the system to their egoistic agenda and this leads to fundamental distortions in the way a community is governed. The main problem is the inability of the rulers to understand the basic needs of the community and to formulate its best interest. Instead they use the community as a tool for their selfish growth. A typical example of such lack of understanding is the allocation of public resources for increasing the standard of living of the rulers on the account of the rest of the citizens in a state. The interest of the community is egoistic societies is disregarded, while the main focus for the rulers is to hold their position of power for as long as possible. When the interests of a community are not well understood and not clearly formulated, the right objectives cannot be set and the participants cannot be organized in a meaningful way. The resources of the community are desired from private corporations or states in order to gain profit and the relevant criteria is using convenient resources and not the most appropriate for satisfying the interests of the whole. A typical example is the use of oil and gas for energy needs, instead of decisive and prompt reorientation of the states and private sector in efficient production of energy from renewable sources.

One of the gravest flaws of the capitalistic model is that the system maintains the opportunity for violation of basic human rights, if this lead to enrichment of well-established participants in the society. We see the application of this statement when labor rights of employees are violated by private companies, especially if they are in the developing countries. In the western countries the obvious misuse of the rights of the employee is monitored much better and such bad practices are "outsourced" when these actions are acceptable and invisible.

Today for everyone is clear that in democratic societies the economically strong groups are having the highest influence in the state what kind of policies should be lead and the scientifically based estimate of the needs of the community is fading away and remains irrelevant. When national interest and state objectives become a compromise between private interests, this would inevitably lead to disregarding of the interests of the whole.

In every country on the planet the working process is organized in such a way that non-governmental employees are forced to act in satisfaction of private interests. This is their chance to receive access to goods and services. In this process it is not necessary employees to be informed about concrete results from their activities and very often they are unaware about the consequences from the overall functioning of the organization. The idea that a man lives and works in order to survive and to prove himself in a social class does not correspond with another idea - being useful for the whole community and demanding your work and energy be directed in service to all humankind, for example.

From the known history of mankind until present day, states have been always functioning as systems in service to the self. Governance in all states, without regards whether their citizens have more or less rights than others, is down to struggle for power and efforts to maintain it. Power, understood as the ability to take something from someone, is the main means for survival of the individual or of small group of people in the egoistic systems. Political organizations are more often organized, so that small groups of people are positioning themselves, in order to guarantee access to public resources at distribution on their own discretion.

Despite these systemic flaws, if we make brief historical review, we will see an evolution in the understanding of the role of the political power and of the ways a society is governed. In Ancient times and in the Middle Ages the political power in most societies was perceived as an absolute right of the monarch (emperor, king, khan, tsar, sultan, etc.) to take decisions on all matters and to delegate his right, given by God. Until the adoption of Magna Carta in 1215 the absolute character of the monarchical power was intact from rights of the subjects in Europe. Later, in XVII, XVIII and especially in XIX century the political power in the Old continent and in America was not just limited by the granted rights to different groups of citizens, but there was a change in the way it was received.

It would be improper and hasty to conclude that the provision of political power through democratic elections leads necessarily to appointing of more capable leaders, who will govern in the interest of the community. The major advantage of democratic governance over transfer of political power via succession is the necessity of dialogue between the rulers and the ruled in which it may (without being mandatory) be regulated the rights of the different social groups. The risk from power abuse and violation of rights continues to exist even when the power is decentralized and it is liberated from its absolute character.

In Europe Montesquieu is trying to solve on a theoretical level the practical problem of abusing of power, by leaning to the democratic model of Ancient Greece. We have to remind that democracy in Ancient Hellas, especially before the times of Solon, did not exclude slavery, did not guarantee the rights of the demos, and could not prevent political usurpation of power. Aristotle describes very clearly what the social relations were from that time: *"loans were secured upon the persons of the debtors, and the land was in the hands of a few"* [13]. This situation remains unchanged until today in all states.

If we move our attention later and review the social relations and development of democracy in the United States in XVIII century, we will see how inhumane and unscrupulous the process of recognition of legal personality was for people from other races and even from other religions. It is enough to remember that only 300 years ago the General Assembly of Colonial Virginia adopted laws, with which it postulates that *"All servants imported and brought into the Country...who were not Christians in their native Country...shall be accounted and be slaves." An act concerning Servants and Slaves"* [14]

The exhausting efforts of African-Americans for abolition of slavery and their struggle for civil rights continued for decades after the United States was already found as a democratic country with its own constitution. Democracy is considered to be a positive social value only in society, which can preserve its higher virtue of humanism.

We can discover similar message about the inter-dependence between social virtues and democracy in the words of Montesquieu, when he describes the problems, which egoistic attitudes cause for democracy and the community:

"The politic Greeks, who lived under a popular government, knew no other support than virtue. (...) When virtue is banished, ambition invades the minds of those who are disposed to receive it, and avarice possesses the whole community. The objects of their desires are changed; what they were fond of before has become indifferent; they were free while under the restraint of laws, but they would fain now be free to act against law; and as each citizen is like a slave who has run away from his master, that which was a maxim of equity he calls rigor;

---

13 The Athenian Constitution; The Internet Classics Archive by Daniel C. Stevenson, Web Atomics

14 October 1705, Hening's Statutes at Large, (Philadelphia: 1823), Vol. 3, Ch. XLIX, 447-462, archived by Crandall Shifflett, Virtual Jamestown, 1998

that which was a rule of action he styles constraint; and to precaution he gives the name of fear" [15]

In reality is there independence between legislative and executive authority, which is stipulated in the democratic parliamentary societies? In other words, can representatives of the executive authority influence the representatives of the legislative one? It is a common knowledge that the leader of ruling parties are stepping into the executive positions, while the lower echelon of the party fill in the seats in the parliament as representatives of legislature. Of course both authorities are not independent, because the legislative representatives are in hierarchical subordination and chosen by the representatives of higher executive positions in the corresponding parties. The private interests of the parties and their influence to the members of Parliament are an obstacle to decision-making in the best pubic interest and therefore another form of dependence of the legislative and executive authorities. Therefore, the principles for determining the social norms, such as the laws of the state, are infiltrated by major egoistic interests, which are dominating the leading parties.

On a theoretical level the judicial authority is positioned in a way that provides the possibility for it to be independent by the other two authorities and by private interests. Whether this would happen depends entirely on the ethics of the people, who are part of the judiciary.

We can conclude that democratic parliamentary governing does not achieve the concentration of power, but displacement of the focus of public awareness on organs, which are not forming policies, but implementing already taken decisions. Political power remains monolithic in this model of state governing, but the places and ways of high-level decision-making remain opaque and without monitoring. The great problem of using positions of power for egoistic private interest is intact and unresolved in the present democratic mechanism of the modern state.

The disadvantages of the democracy are quite well-known, but it is unpopular to be discussed and criticized, because this form of choosing of leadership is convenient to those, who are able to form public attitudes and swing public opinion.

---

15 Baron de Montesquieu, *The spirit of Laws*, 1748, p.26

Here we have to stress that in states, where fair democratic elections do not exist there is much more often violation of human rights and political power is preserved with brutal means and suppression of the population. It would be much more difficult to transform such societies to be in service to the whole, because their citizens do not have so many freedoms.

The main infirmity in governing in all democratic states is that the dominating private interests are presented to be public, in order to be justified specific selfish behavior. Examples include privileged funding for big corporations, because they are considered "too big to fall"; political lobbying on their behalf in international relations, undermining fundamental rights of people and the environment in order to protect the profits of a few private subjects. The necessity to choose leadership in a democratic community, in order to be taken a direction for development, is reduced to comparison of the striving of different parties and people to survive and the efforts, they are prepared to make in order to persuade their electorate. The political power is a prize for these efforts and not a logical conclusion of good governmental thinking. Conversion of power into political and economic reward for the efforts of a group of people to gain the trust of a larger electorate is another great obstacle for building good governance in democratic societies! Because of these conditions of choosing leadership, the attitudes, values, actions and skills of those, who are struggling for power in state elections are such that the system will rise a winner in a contest and not a capable manager, who understand in-depth the needs of the community and who has the qualities to organize a large group of people to satisfy these need, while at the same time protects the interests of the whole.

Another flaw of the contemporary ways of conducting democratic parliamentary or presidential elections, which adjustment would be very difficult, is that the quantitative criteria for election in modern democratic societies leads to qualitative problems in governing.

Despite that democracy is a much developed form of peaceful selection of leadership and political representation than the bloodbath between clans and social classes, it validates the selfish intentions of a small group of people to gain power and not their real capacity for satisfying the interests of the society. We should make a fair conclusion that the modern democratic model finds the answer of the question "Who is the most determined to gain power and is ready to be compliant with the dominating private interests?" and not of the question "Which organization or person is most capable to govern a specific field?"

The notion of a competition of ideas in a free and informed society is already reduced to an election of convenient representatives compliant to corporate interests and people are forced to choose a lesser evil. What is important in this process is that it is not a decline or a deviation of the democratic model, but its natural effect and logical continuation of its implementation, when leading is the principle "survival of the fittest" and the environment is insecure. The reason for this decline can be traced in the economic inequality, which is maintained by capitalism, and its intrinsic deformation of the purpose of human existence and the motivation of creating goods. Most of the people are looking at the political power as a spectacle in which they have a small role of a voter in an election. Such a distanced attitude towards community development has been formed, because the regular people are compelled to think and act almost exclusively for the prosperity of themselves and their families. Completely different is the attitude of the big corporations, for which political power is the best means for their survival and prosperity. Precisely the representatives of the big corporations understand and are taught to outlive in a competitive environment by adapting the system to themselves step by step; by entering in strategic alliances and by using the needs of different groups of people. These large private subjects in the Western democracies have paved the road to political power and they would let only those who are ready to comply with corporate interests, instead with those of the respective nation. Through financing and media influence they can boost a political project and jeopardize another, depending on their whim.

In the process of its growth the big corporation always reaches the conclusion that its sustainability, prosperity and security are dependent on its influence to state governing and to international relations. This is a logic step of "investment" on behalf of every big corporation, because political influence means better control on income and costs, as well as protection of its private interests on the international stage.

The income of the big corporation is dependent from the market, the extent of impact over its customers, the quality of the goods and their price. The due taxes to the state, the regulations and business climate are highly affected of the policies of the state in which the corporation is functioning. Therefore, it is a natural habit of a well-established private actor to use different instruments to make attempts to influence political decisions and even to form state policies.

Secondly, the corporations concreted their relationship with the state by the fact that they are creating most of the jobs and maintain control of the access to goods for most of the people. Remuneration and not the service to society is the main motivational force to apply for a working position in a corporation or in governmental structure.

In the egoistic systems the creation of a working position itself is considered a political success and state's officials and political leaders are not interested in the employee's level of satisfaction, his desired personal development, sufficient free time and whether he has decent access to economic goods.

The holistic organization is obliged to consider all these factors, because the employees are those representatives of humankind for whom the organization is supposed to act in their interest.

The third solid relationship between a collective of corporations and the state power is related with the financial system and particularly acquiring of influence over printing of money and determining the interest rates. This means that private companies will be able to devaluate labor, commodities or assets on their discretion. If this activities are privatized the social development is dependent to a large extent from the selfish intentions of those big corporations, which are shaping not only the economic system, but also the financial one. This type of collaboration between state power and large capitalists leads to the following global problem: every activity which brings profit for the private organizations, without regards whether it is harmful for humankind and for other species, will be carried out. The weakness of separate individuals to counteract and the artificial maintained perception of division between them make these problems hard to overcome, but not unresolvable.

Holistic governing in its ideal form

Many forms and variations of the holistic model for governing can be created and they may be working well enough for satisfying the interests of the whole. However, they all should have one common characteristic and it is the aim of governing.

The aim of the holistic governing is the organization to satisfy in the best possible way the interests of the subjects of the holistic model and by integrating them - the interest of the whole. This means that the management team should plan the production and distribution processes of the goods from public property in a way which does not harm the environment, does not lead to depletion of Earth's resources and does not violate drastically the rights of all living beings.

The overall policy of the holistic organization and its economic functioning should be following this main aim. It is not enough one organization to produce more and more goods and to realize bigger profits, in order to be determined that it is working properly which are the criteria in the capitalistic system.

The primordial purpose of every state is to protect the identity of the corresponding nation, its cultural characteristics and population, by creating the prerequisites of a joyful life of its citizens. The holistic approach in the economic relations would be beneficial for even greater achievements of these national ideals. This governing approach includes building of an environment, which is supporting the creativity of its participants and exercising of their free will in a way which protects the interests of the whole. The holistic governance foresees decentralized decision-making which is supported by global planning for the provision of the needed resources.

Decentralized systems and network structures with high autonomy succeed to function better, because they are able to take local decisions for implementing global aims. When a local leader or management team are responsible for the development of the organization and understand in-depth the specifics and needs of the particular region, they are able to form concrete solutions of different problems and to chart a way of development of the organization. The exercising of this free will develops the managing skills of the local organization, and provides the opportunity of the most appropriate building of relationships with other subjects, which are based on direct knowledge of the environment. These principles are implemented to a large extend in modern social systems. The difference in the holistic model is that all local branches are supplied with needed material resources, which are produced by the central governing authority. This premise is needed, because only after global planning of the production and logistics of resources can be performed all necessary actions to satisfy the interests of the whole. Tender procedures and contracting of small-scale private suppliers, which are interested in lower costs and higher profits is typical for the capitalistic society.

Global governance of resources on every stage for supplying the needs of local structures will lead to huge reduction of costs; to less contamination of the environment; to integration of different economic fields; to preserving of high-level access to goods for all employees on the chain and the possibility to achieve all other requirements for satisfying the interests of the whole. These results could never be achieved even by the biggest corporation, which is socially responsible and ecologically matured, because of the competitive environment that it is functioning.

If holistic governing is implemented by public institutions, it will expand tremendously the understanding of the functions of the state authority from the one that is prevailing in the egoistic systems. It would not be an opportunity to dictate, or even suppress your subordinates, but a responsibility for provision of instruments for raising their awareness and encouraging they are active involvement. Holistic governing focuses on proper transfer of knowledge to the subjects, which should help them be responsible for themselves and be responsible in the building of relationships with others. This understanding of the power requires that the governor is capable to adapt they system constantly towards the positive creative endeavors and initiatives of the citizens and not towards himself, or towards different parties and groups of corporations. Therefore, this quality is not just audibility of the ruling elite or a dialogue with the citizens on specific topics, but a real service directed to fulfill those creative potential of the participants, which is aimed to satisfy the interests of the whole. In order to be present these initiatives and intelligent decision-making on different topics, the holistic organization should constantly improve the conditions for development of its participants.

Egoistic societies, on the other hand, have a completely different aim. They are purpose is to control the participants and to stimulate them to produce more and more. In order to achieve that, they should not develop the "dangerous" habit to raise legitimate questions about the defects of the social system and even "more dangerous" one to find meaningful answers for themselves.

Every holistic organization needs to develop itself from bottom up - from free citizens, who are expressing their will to live in service to the whole. Every organization functions through its organs and therefore it is necessary to exist a selection process of the people, who are going to govern. The holistic model differentiates from the egoistic one also that the management team is willing to prepare the participants in the system to understand the needs of the community and to raise their awareness of the interests of the whole. It is necessary, because those people, who are most qualified in the specific areas and are ready to be bare responsibility, are going to be appointed for the related positions and are going to form the policies. It is necessary electors and elected people to be prepared excellently, in order to be determined the most appropriate people for certain governing position.

In modern democratic societies the rating is the sacred cow for a politician, without regards what kind of electorate stands behind it, without regards what the ideas and promises are behind this rating. This state of dependence from the public opinion and from the momentary attitudes distorts the scientifically based problem-solving in the interests of the whole, without regards what part of the population understands these problems and how many people would support working decisions. Dooming the political power to be dependent on public opinion leads only to the conclusion that those, who are capable to guide it, generate certain reality for the rest and in practice they influence their decisions and indirectly choose who will be in power. This type of influence demonstrates again how selfish private interests are able to navigate the management of public resources, by using the weaknesses of the modern social systems.

The application of the holistic model into the state governing will lead to reduction of the competitiveness and power struggle and their substitution with competition for political position and election, based on merit. It is surprising why in parliamentary democracies it is foreseen to apply competitions and interviews for all governmental positions in order to select the most appropriate person, except for the highest positions, which are considered to be "political appointments". Aren't they the most important positions for good governance and aren't they supposed to be hold by the most qualified professionals?!

In the holistic organization all participants are included in the decision-making process of different sectors of the system. They freely choose the field in which to be professionally trained and the work that they desire to perform and build a career. During the whole working process they are free to decide whether to abide by a decision, chosen as the best one for a certain project.

It is important to emphasize that the sum of all private interests does not represent the interests of the whole! As was written above, the holistic system perceives humans, animals, plants and the Earth as spiritual beings who are part of the whole and therefore all social processes should be organized in a way which is corresponding to their spiritual development(awareness of being connected with the Absolute).

In order to be chosen the most appropriate manager for a particular sector of the holistic organization, it is necessary the candidate to be the most prepared one to understand the interests of the whole and to know the ways for developing the specific area. This can be achieved by applying the already known methods for selection: holding of competition, tests, interviews, etc.

Therefore the electoral system of a holistic organization provides the opportunity for everyone to participate, but is structured in a way to be selected the most qualified person to manage certain professional area. Lobbying in the holistic organization and economic dependence of the management is in contradiction with the purpose of these organizations, because egoistic attitudes are introduced in decision-making. It can be concluded that governing of a holistic organization is considered to be an expert activity on a higher level and there is no opposition between expert and political decision, which is present in the present-day capitalistic and communistic systems.

The holistic organization should carry out the selection in such a way, that egoistic motives for attaining and holding power are avoided.

The holistic approach of governance is completely opposite to the capitalistic one, because the main motivation to include people in a working process is their inspiration for desired self-expression in service to the community and in the interest of the whole.

The next step in guaranteeing good governance of the organization is making management activities to be unattractive occupation for people with selfish ambitions and full of greed. This is conducted by eliminating the opportunities for profit and privileges, which contemporary political power provides for the ruler directly, or to the people, who are close to him. In egoistic systems the political power is reduced to the right to determine who is going to receive more goods than others, and how much the state should take from different groups and persons. In more free societies have been drawn out criteria for a dignified payment and principles for good governance and budgeting. In these states the ruling party has the possibilities to influence significantly to the economic processes in someone's favor. The rulers are capable to change the tax policies which mean to choose which participant will have less, in order to fill the state budget. They are able to implement policies, which can lead to diminishing of someone's property. The mere possibility of the rulers to change the tax policies of the state creates uncertainty for the private persons. The result of this uncertainty is fear for their survival and prosperity and this makes political power in necessary means for the big private corporations, which are willing to be in control of the situation.

It is well known that the rulers in the egoistic systems have the right to choose for what purpose to be used the public resources and which private organizations to profit from their exploitation.

Unlike the egoistic system, the holistic one is structured in a way, which prohibits the possibility of the rulers to redistribute most of the public property at their discretion. Their task is to put in practice the principle of equal access to public goods which are due and distributed to the participants as a form of right and not sold as merchandise. Such access to public property is not dependent from the profession, the level of occupied position, nor even to the quality of work of the participant, because public goods are not used as a reward, but as due right. This is how good governance of the holistic organization will lead to more quality products for the whole community and not for a small group of privileged people.

The second guarantee for the creation of harmonious and secure environment in a holistic organization, which is functioning in the ideal holistic model, is the elimination of the possibility to take private resources as a form of state tax. In case of partial implementation of the holistic model in capitalistic states, it would mean fixing the tax burden for private citizens and making changes of the taxes only after an agreement with the affected party.

Is it possible to achieve good state governance, which is not dependent on the income in the form of taxes from private subjects? Such a step seems unthinkable in the modern understanding of the functions of the state. To large extent the state has abandoned its role of creating economic products and to provide goods and services to its population. Most of the states do not provide to their population neither the accommodation, nor the food, the automobiles, the fuel for them, nor any of the pallets of services, which are available today. The way a modern state is functioning presently is to divide the society by maintaining of permanent competition and collecting taxes from the products, which private citizens are selling to each other. As it is well known the state is responsible to use these tax collections to provide other services, such as judiciary, national defense, education, healthcare, foreign policy and many others, but not the basic needs of the population.

In the holistic model of social organizing every participant has the right to receive access to certain public goods and services in sufficient quantity and optimal quality. This form of distribution of public property must be with equal access to all participants, as it is described in chapter five. In the scope of distributed public goods are included also those of first necessity.

The detailed description of clear principles for distribution of goods leads to elimination or at least strong limitation of the possibilities to misuse power and public office. If for the public official is lacking the opportunity to distribute goods or to regulate taxing policies, it would result in diminishing of the magnetic attraction to political power for people, who are driven from greed and selfishness. This magnetism is very strong in the egoistic societies throughout the known history. Therefore, combatting the misuse of power is conducted not by its decentralization, rotation, or provision to a group of people, instead of one person. All these characteristics are implemented in every modern state, but they do not diminish the risks from misuse, but reduce the opportunity to correspondingly excessive, long-term, or sole misuse of power. The division and deconcentration of power gives birth to oligarchic structures and oligopoly economic relationships and not to protection of human rights and interests of humankind.

Holistic governing aims to eliminate the actual negative characteristics of power and to reduce the risk of misusing of official positions by introducing the following principles:

1. Adopting of hardly changeable rules for distribution of public goods, guaranteeing equal and free access to all participants. None of the participants should have the right to receive bigger or lesser access to public goods, without regards his status in the system, because this form of distribution is exercising of a right and not a form of reward, or sanction. None of the participants of the holistic organization can receive fewer amounts of goods and services, comparing with the past, as well as less freedoms in relation with the others, without his consent. Distribution of public goods should be performed by application of already approved algorithm, which purpose is to reply optimally to the needs and desires of the consumers, without maintaining privileges.

2. It introduces detailed job description for occupying a position, especially with regards to higher governmental political ones. Official job positions, which in the egoistic societies are considered as political and are supposed to reflect the interests of the ruling party, in a holistic society are considered as expert. In the last occupation of a higher office position is not on the basis of party merits or compliance with leading corporate interests, but should be achieved after a competition and precise in-depth evaluation of the ethics of the person, his experience and his decision-making abilities to satisfy the interests of the subjects of the holistic model. The organs of the state, which are political official positions, should not have the authority to appoint people who are not the best prepared for a specific position and selected after a competition.

Every decision, taken by an employee, should me motivated, in order to be established whether it would be satisfied the interest of the whole. This prerequisite is necessary also to determine the way of thinking of the particular employee and to provide the opportunity for the people, who are going to be affected by the decision to be informed of its purpose.

3. It tries to eliminate the possibility political power to be used for violation of human rights (including the equal access to public goods) of the participants of the holistic organization, without regards the threats for the society. In modern states threats for national security are used as convenient excuse for eavesdrop, surveillance, detention without charges, torture, inhumane treatment during interrogation and even initiating a war with mock enemy. The existence of some enemy is a necessity and a prerequisite for investing in national security systems. Holistic organizations must never betray the principle of humanity, which is fundamental for their creation, without regards the threats for society. Committing or indirectly supporting activities, which violate human rights, must be prohibited in every holistic organization. When there is a need of the community, which may affect the rights of the participants, it is necessary to be found alternative methods and ways of satisfying that need. If it is impossible for the management team to find such alternatives, consent of the affected people is needed, before initiating these actions.

Holistic council

The application of the holistic model in an organization, which had declared that will function in the service to the whole, should lead to according change of its governing organs and structure. It is necessary in order to be protected the interest of the holistic model by creating the environment for their improved integration. An example of such collective governing organ is the **holistic council**. Presently this organ should include representation of the interests of the four subjects of the holistic model: humankind, animals, plants and Earth. If the activity of the organization is affecting other celestial bodies or extraterrestrial living beings, their interests should also be taken into consideration by the council.

In the process of reviewing project plans, everyone from the representatives of the holistic council prepares a brief report, which includes evaluation of the risks that would emerge for the corresponding subject, in the process of the realization of the project. Despite describing the problematic interventions and violation of interests of the subjects, the representatives should point out the possible ways of avoiding them and to propose a way of achieving optimal satisfaction of the interests.

The representatives of the holistic council perceive the whole through the prism of the subject, they are representing, and they are not fixes in one-sided protection of the corresponding interests on the account of all others.

Depending on the planned activity and who is the main subject of the holistic model, towards whom it is directed, the corresponding representative has a leading role in the organ and should prepare a final report and action plan. In this final report is supposed to be formulated the optimal way of satisfying the interests of the subjects of the holistic model and from there - those of the whole.

Let's take for example the building of residential building in a city and the functioning of a holistic council on a municipality level. This activity is conducted mostly for satisfying the interests of the human-kind and therefore his representative in the council has a leading role in managing the council and he is responsible for the preparation of the final report and the action plan.

The representative of the interests of the humankind should bring out all the components of the construction activities, which has to make the building in the best possible living place for the local people. These are the choice for location, quality of construction, optimal area, quality of sewer and water network, electricity, heating and all other indicators which will make the project with optimal high quality. In order to be protected the interests of the Earth and the environment, the representa-tive of the interests of the planet would be responsible for choosing the most suitable territory for construction, the best ecological practices, the activities which guarantee lowest level of air pollution and propos-als of different forms of prevention of all forms of contamination.

The representative of the interests of the animals should analyze whether the construction of the building effects negatively to some of the animal species in the region and if so to propose a solution for the problem. The apologist of the plants should also research and evaluate from the perspective of the interest of the flora and if the construction would harm species, he should propose a solution.

After every member of the council presents his report, the proce-dure moves to discussion how to be avoided or mitigated the foreseen violation of interests. If harmful activities cannot be avoided in that time, the council should find a way to restrict them and make them as less damaging as possible. In order to be effective, the holistic council should apply mechanisms for avoidance of deadlock points of moving the process, because there is lacking of cooperative attitude to integrate the interests.

Such a mechanism is the possibility for making proposals for avoiding specific violations of interests. They can be made by all members of the council and not just in relation to the subject, they are representing. The introduction of this right is very important for the proper functioning of the organization, because it is very likely the representatives of the interests of one subject not to realize that with certain activities they are violating the interests of other subjects. Such lack of awareness is logical to exist in the beginning, because most probably they do not know the interests of other living beings, what is important for them and how to avoid damages. The purpose of the holistic council is in mutual enrichment with perspectives and in raising the awareness of all members and the organization in general in relation to initiation of every project. The added knowledge of affecting the interests of the others is basic prerequisite for making the optimal strategy of the project, but it cannot guarantee that the decision-making process will be evolved. This is why a second mechanism is needed, which should be related with the hierarchy of the interests of the subjects.

In this hierarchy the interests of the Earth are standing higher than all other three subjects, followed by the interests of humankind, those of the animal kingdom and finally the plants. The main criterion for taking a decision in the interest of the whole is related with the good integration and optimal satisfaction of the needs of the subjects. After discussing the viewpoints and the different positive and negative effects from the proposed activities, the leading representative is summarizing them and prepares the final report. In this document is substantiated the proposed decision and the reasons why it is optimal version to satisfy the interests of the whole.

The third mechanism is related with the opportunity of a council member to substantiate and propose a better decision and more inclusive solution of the faced challenges. Right of every member of the council is to make an overall proposal for better integration of the interests. If the decision is accepted by the leading member, it is incorporated in the final report.

After everyone had received the opportunity to present their motivated proposal for better protection of the interest of the whole, the council moves to voting of the final report. Every member has one vote and the vote against the proposed version should be followed by an additional constructive proposal for change.

If the governing system of the holistic organization is structured on several levels, for every member who does not agree with a proposal should exist the opportunity to present an appeal on a higher holistic council, which should review whether there is a better solution. This approach provides a guarantee that in cases of excessive violation of the interests of a subject of the holistic model, it would be known by other holistic councils in the organization. In this way it would be possible for searching of more inclusive decisions of a specific case from a higher perspective.

How to determine the most appropriate person for an official position?

For every office position, including and especially for the higher governmental, the choice should be made on the basis of transparent criteria, which have to stand out the most prepared candidate, who would be capable to lead social policies in a way which protects the interest of the whole. In order to be certain that such choice would be made, it is necessary the candidates to be selected impartially and expertly. The holistic system does not divide the participants into viewers (citizens), actors (politicians) and scriptwriters (actors behind the political scenes) and it is not build to provide the whole legislative and executive power to one party or a coalition for certain period of time.

The egoistic systems introduce the competition process for almost all of the expert positions, except the most significant ones- the political. Placing of convenient people on higher positions, without necessarily having the required qualities, experience and ethics, is needed for those forces, close to power, that would be capable of influencing these people.

For the holistic management of the community is typical that all participants are included in the system through their activities and capabilities for development in the desired area. When a person gain experience in a professional area, he would understand better what are its needs and he would be better prepared to know who is capable to form large-scale political vision in this field, which protects the interests of the whole. Therefore, it is logical this person to be given the opportunity to choose among the candidates in a specific field. This precondition for sectorial choice by professionals should be differentiated from the election qualification, which was typical in several forms of democratic elections.

In the holistic community every adult person chooses a field of expertise in which he desires to develops his skills and gain knowledge. Precisely in this field it is logical this person to be able to exercise freely his voting rights for a particular electoral position. The difference with the democratic elections in the egoistic societies is that people would participate in elections only in the sector, which they are professionally involved in. The election is supposed to be for a particular person with his views and competencies and not for a party, which is going to control and direct its representative and that will lobby for particular political decisions. The advantage of such sectorial election over the general one is that the voters would be much more informed about the priorities and challenges in the specific area and this will result in stimulation of the candidates to present detailed visions for development. A possible defect would be professional differentiation to lead to guild capsulation and this may result in egoistic attitudes of professional classes. In order to be avoided such a challenge, it is important to be created deep and strong relations between the different sectors.

How to be avoided the abuse of power and misuse of official position?

When mentioning abuse of office most often it is meant taking advantage from an official position to procure benefits for himself or others. This form of dishonest behavior is typical for every government in the world, without exception. However, there is another more dangerous form of abuse of power and it is the replacement of the national interests with selfish private interests. If the first kind of abuse is leading to partial violation of public interests and misappropriation of public property, the second is affecting negatively the direction of development of society, by blocking or eliminating the creative initiatives for good governance in the service of the nation. Many political leaders are using national interests as a screen, behind which are visible characteristics like greed, inhumanity, desire for dominance and cruelty.

The perishing of human lives and the waste of natural resources in wars, which are violating the interests of humankind and are creating tensions of international relations, is one of the most visible examples for misuse of political power.

The holistic system aims to avoid all forms of misuse of political power and official positions and applies very different approach in relation to egoistic systems. In order to achieve good policy making, material stimulus and deprivations should not be used to influence the motivation, discipline and the loyalty of the respective person on the official position.

The main purpose of the management of a holistic organization is to inspire the participants to perform useful work, they desire, in a cooperative and not competitive manner, in order to satisfy the interests of the whole. Unlike the governance in an egoistic organization, the holistic system cannot be directed to violate rights of a person or a group of people, without regards what he has done. Poverty of a participant in a holistic organization can be only by his own choice, because if there are local or global economic difficulties, they would be met with equal weight by all participants. Therefore, it would not be necessary to survive on the expense of someone's personal rights and dignity, as it is occurring in the service to self systems. An important part of the management of a particular community is choosing a direction for development. The holistic organizations are going to have much more clearly defined aim than the egoistic capitalistic and communistic societies, which are directed towards their survival on the expense of others. Holistic governance is considering the freedom of the participants to choose whether to be part of certain process and respect their right to be informed about it from early stage planning to the evaluation of results. These freedoms substantiate governing methods to be through inspiration to include those, who are willing and capable to perform certain tasks. Another important difference with the egoistic systems is the necessity of concurrence of will of all participants in the process of its implementation.

The principles of free participation and transparency of the activities in the holistic organization require completely different approach of governance in relation to imperativeness.

Holistic governance reduces the imperativeness of higher authorities. The egoistic organizations create their own stability, depending on the rule that the decisions of higher authorities will be imposed over the ruled and if they are not obeyed, this will result in sanctions. Obviously, such people are not free, if they have to carry out decisions from higher authorities, for which they did not expressed their consent.

Is it possible to achieve good governance and organizational stability, by preserving the relative autonomy of the individual to take decisions on various issues and to express consent on every decision of authority, which affects him? The holistic system is built exactly on those principles and therefore the answer of the question is affirmative.

In the organizations, created on holistic model, there would also be hierarchy, but the higher authority would be responsible to govern the borders of exercising free will of the participants for which he is responsible. This will result in much greater freedom for them to choose the path of own development and at the same time would be protected the rights and freedoms of the others. This is a significant distinction of governing methods between both types of systems. Egoistic organizations use everyone, who is lower in the hierarchy as a figurine without freedom and as a resource for personal use. It is precisely the use free will, which gives meaning to person's life, shows him who he is in reality and provides him with the opportunity to develop personally through taking responsibilities

The management of the holistic organizations would count on the free participation of all participants and on the personal negotiation with the organization about the rights and duties that are expected from both sides - the organization and the participant. The role of the leadership is much more related to positively inspire the participants, explain the common goals of the organization and serve as an example of how to live in service to the whole. The expert qualities of the people who are responsible to organize certain process and to take decisions in certain field are the strongest motivational factor for other participants to trust the judgment of the leadership and to be inspired to co-work with them. Higher ethics and professionalism of the leadership are supposed to gain respect of the relevant institution, to which they belong and to the system, which were capable to identify these people, educate and prepare them to solve the challenges in front of the community. The egoistic systems are reversed to this logic and they require respect and obedience to the institutions, without regards from the qualities of their representatives and the overall results of their work. In these societies is demanded subjection to the imposed rules, even though that they might be inhumane, unjust and not working. Even if they are such rules, they still remain outwardly imposed and not agreed, because of the imperativeness in the state law.

The holistic organization provides the opportunity of the participants of the organization to evaluate its employee from all levels on the basis of their actual skills, knowledge and deeds. Those people, who have achieved the best results and are the most capable have the right to take the corresponding official position in the holistic organization, including the higher political ones.

An official of a holistic organization may expect to gain the respect of the community only if he deserves this with his own actions and not by the office per se. This will require much more efforts from the person to be prepared to take good decisions for the community and in the interest of the whole. Contrary to this principle, in the egoistic systems is foreseen that orders from higher authority should be executed blindly and the responsibility is not personal, but it is transferred to the superior. This transfer of responsibility in the egoistic hierarchical systems is validating that the participants are not free and are considered as a mere resource for implementing policies. Such lack of responsibility of the people does not lead to clearing their consciousness of a psychologically healthy person, if he was executing orders, which have led to adverse changes and violation of the interests of the whole. Typical example is selfish military invasions in states, which result in total devastation, murders and other inhumane acts, and the performers of these actions are merely people, who are following orders in a selfish hierarchical structure.

An important feature of the holistic governance is that the refusal to execute an official order, because of ethical or other concerns, does not lead to sanctions, including deprivation of access to goods. In the absence of fear for losing his job, which is the main source of goods, the freedom of the person to constantly compare the principles of every project he is invited to participate and his own ethics is much bigger. Therefore, the higher ethics of the individual will result into guarantee for good governance of the organization. It is the ethics of service to the whole that is of primal importance in the education of the people in a holistic system.

If a soldier is not convinced in the cause of a particular military intervention, he should have the right to ask more detailed information, in order to evaluate whether he would like to participate in it or not. Such freedom of the people is unthinkable for the states as we know them from the past until modern days.

The political power in egoistic system is reduced to the opportunity of one person to deprive another from rights and to change in a negative way his development. In holistic governance the power is a form of trust from the community towards a person to find the best solutions, to inspire the other participants and to develop the organization, so that it can serve the interests of the whole.

How is changed the labor process in applying holistic governance?

The role of the labor process and the principles of using labor force are extensive topic, which is separately reviewed in more detail in chapter 6, while here are presented what are the major shifts in perception of the labor from egoistic to holistic governance.

Every working activity of a project requires precise planning of all resources. Among these resources is human labor and managing people. Egoistic systems are built in such a way, so that all employees should provide the maximum working force for maximum amount of time, which is in the interest of the organizations, exploiting the people. Eight hours working time is adopted as a normal continuation, in order to push to the maximum the economic system and it serves the interests of corporations and states and not the individual and humankind. Free time is planned in such a way, so that it is the perfect pause for "recharging" of the human organism and the people start over with new strength their work.

The holistic approach reviews working time of the employee as a chosen form of expression and right to participate in a desired project, which serves the interests of the whole. In the holistic system the person should be able to work for a minimum necessary time, so that can be achieved the set objectives. In an organization in service to the whole free time is not regarded as needed for regaining of strength, but as an opportunity of the person to be truly free to live, create, explore and perform all other activities that he enjoys.

The mandatory working time for the employee is the one, without which the system would not be able to function properly, because it would not be possible to create and provide the needed goods and services to the participants. If a particular employee desires to continue to perform his working activities more than the foreseen minimum, it is part of his voluntary working time, which does not bring him additional remuneration, access to goods, or privileges.

Holistic governance of the labor process means that the pace and pressure of developing the economic system should be set in the interest of the people, who are at the same time employees and consumers. Therefore, the mandatory working time for the system should not hinder the person's social contacts, entertainments and his time for participation in other projects. Respecting the free time of the person most probably will determine mandatory working time between four to six hours a day in a five-day workweek. Every particular holistic organization should determine the specific continuation of the working time, without exceeding the legally adopted requirements of the state, it is functioning. The holistic organizations are supposed to make this decision well-grounded and based on a serious research on the issue.

What are the principles to correct unlawful behavior of a participant in a holistic organization?

In the egoistic systems specific behavior is demanded, and deviation from it results in punishing the person, who is breaching the norm, while in the systems of service to the whole a focus is placed on clarifying the necessity of certain behavior. On the basis of contract, the participant of the holistic organization declares that he accepts the goals and the principles of the organization, in order to receive the right to be part of it and to have access to all goods and services. The expressed statement on behalf of the participant is a manifestation of his freedom to accept or not the basic norms and principles of the holistic community. For this reason the organization is not acting repressively upon a participant, who has violated the legal norms, but works with him and encourages him to fulfill his declaration that he is obliged to abide by these norms.

In every society it is completely "normal" violation of socially accepted norms of behavior to occur. For the holistic organization is of crucial importance why certain deviation is made: is it because the person does not realize that he is damaging the society; is it because he neglects the damages, because his aim is to achieve certain good for himself; is it because the violation of norms were necessary, because they were not accurately formed and need further development. There are many more reasons for unlawful behavior and the holistic organization is interested from all of them.

The legislation of a state, which has adopted the holistic model, is not understood as set of rules, submitting the subjects in the state, but as a freely accepted norms, which have the aim to protect the freedoms of everyone in a way which is respectful to the rights and freedom of the others.

The violation of the norms of a holistic state is bringing the negative effect for the person by itself and it is not necessary to punish him with additional sanctions. Such person had already damaged a social bond, which could have brought him satisfaction and development. Punishment would mean to break the arm of a person, who had broken his other arm by himself.

The focus in holistic governance is placed upon reaching the awareness of not hurting social relationships, because these acts are hindering personal and community development. For the holistic organization it is important that the reason for avoiding such violations of norms is not because of the fear of punishment, but because of respecting the community and the others. Nourishing the natural humane attitudes of the person is main feature of the holistic approach of governance. This is the first step of explaining the interconnectedness of the whole. Therefore, true correctional behavior should not include sanctions of the ego of the person, but this is the pattern of criminal justice for thousands of years. Instead, the holistic society is going to use the institute of humane restorative reaction, which is presented in chapter seven.

Some of the main differences between the governance in egoistic and in holistic systems are summarized in the table below:

	Governance, intrinsic for egoistic system	Governance, intrinsic for holistic system
Mission of the organization	Survival of the organization on the account of the participants, the environment and other organizations	Developing of the whole
Economic environment	Competition, uncertainty and limited access to goods for different classes of people	Protected, cooperative, ecological, equal access to public goods for all
Legal regime	Norms are imposed over the participant; no regards whether he is informed about the basic principles; no need for expressing a consent	The participant is informed about the basic principles; freely chooses whether he accepts to observe them
Motivation of the employee to participate	Survival and economic prosperity; dependent on evaluation of his labor	Participation in projects to develop the whole and himself
The will of the superior	Absolute imperative	Mostly consensual
Informing employees about the activities of the organization	It is not mandatory to inform the employee for what purposes the resources are used	It is mandatory to inform the employee for what purposes the resources are used
Aim to include the participant in the labor process	Using his labor force to achieve profit	Developing the project; developing the person in balance with his other needs
Mandatory working time	8 - 12 hours/day	Maximum 6 hours/day
Stimulus of the employee	Material stimulus	Development of the whole, personal development

CHAPTER 5

HOLISTIC ECONOMY

Every thoroughly build modes of social organization of society should examine economic relationships and principles in the corresponding system. These are the rights of ownership, commercial rules, economic and labor rights and many others.

In continuation of millenniums states have trusted upon different forms of capitalistic economy, in which selfish strive towards fortune is supposed to lead to economic prosperity and the state and private organizations are capable to implement their policies and projects. This is deeply ingrained psychological program how to build economic relationships and how to perceive others as resource, without regards whether they are consumers, economic partners, or competitors. The open in-depth analysis of this pattern or searching an alternative is mildly unpopular endeavors.

Capitalism is related with free economic initiative and the emerging entrepreneurs. If we observe the boundaries of this freedom, we will easily establish the following limitations in capitalistic economy:

● The beginning entrepreneur by definition does not have enough resources, with which he can carry out his project. Therefore he needs an investor or financial credit, which means gaining the trust of private organizations with capital, which are interested in making a profit from it. The result is that the creative impulse of the person to improve society is limited to developing a product, which somebody is ready to purchase at this very moment. Such a product might not be the object that he desires to create in the beginning. The creative impulse has to be merchandized and distorted in accordance to the market, if it wants to prevail in a capitalistic society.

● The freedom of the entrepreneur is extremely limited also by the attitude of the other merchants. Every small or medium enterprise comparatively easily can be forced to merge with a bigger one, which means to lose control over its development. Its relative freedom in the market exists until the moment that it becomes an attractive bite or unattractive competitor for a bigger corporation.

Holistic governing directs economic and social processes globally from a much higher perspective and with completely different aim - to develop the maximum potential of every participant to be creative in the service to the whole. Such projects are planned several decades ahead in order to be beneficial for the participants, but also for the next generations. Here we can stress again that interests of humankind include leaving better environment for the next generations and not exploiting as much as you can sell, as it is in capitalism today. In capitalistic management it is typical that most of the private subjects are making short-term plans and caring for Earth and its species is very often a luxury, or considered to be an obligation of the state or NGOs. The private business is functioning in harsh competition and his aim is to survive by exploiting all available resources in the most profitable way, in order to gain capital, return their debts and pay their taxes. Capitalistic economy is able to function only if the person is identifying himself with his ego and succumbs to its impulses for indulgence. The present day system persuades the individual that his significance as a citizen and as an individual is measured through his material wealth. This attitude is crucial in the formation of demand and supply of new and more luxurious goods. Socio-economic development of individuals and organizations in the capitalistic system is possible, when they are chasing the financial resources and trying to dominate the others. Capitalism encourages creating goods, which can be sold and the person can profit from them, without regards how damaging these products can be, or whether the same resources can be used for much beneficial, ecological and healthy products.

Building of social and political weight of people and organizations with selfish attitudes drastically diminishes the capacity of good leadership in society. On the other hand, people, who perceive themselves as spiritual beings, who are supposed to cherish and care for their emotions, thoughts, actions and values, are becoming inconvenient consumers, who are creating qualitatively different demand. Spirituality which is not related to religious institution and submissive behavior is also resulting in conscious behavior as active citizen and consumer. Such people will understand when they are deceived by politicians, cheated by merchants and misled by religious authorities. If people are living in a moderate and balance way, which does not stimulate others to produce unhealthy or not so needed goods and services, this will result in a small change of direction of the spin of the economic wheel. A person or a group of people, who are led by the driving force of service to the whole, should guarantee their material economic independence, physical security and accurate interaction in the world, in order to see the flourishing of their ideals.

The holistic view does not regard economic abundance and wealth as inhumane status or selfish desires. The social problem emerges, when a person stops to be interested in the effects of his actions, in the process of gaining wealth and starts disregarding the interests of others. Such blindness and selfishness is the biggest social problem of the capitalistic societies and of the economic processes in them!

In order to build the ideal of holistic society, which is capable to function in the interest of the whole and to develop all its members in the direction, they desire and in harmony with the environment, it is necessary to provide and answer of the following question: *How to create holistic economy?*

Presently, all states are structuring their economies, applying the egoistic capitalistic model. This means that in order to be applied the holistic economic model, it has to be introduced in such a way, so that it can adapt in the beginning to the capitalistic system of relationships. The reason for applying the holistic economic model as part of the capitalistic societies is because there is no political and economic vacuum on the planet. The possibilities for experimenting variations of the holistic economic model are open with the discovering of new lands. This hypothesis is applicable mainly in outer space exploration, because Earth has already been distributed to different nations. Here it is important to highlight that in the past "the discovery" of new lands was most of the time their taking away from the native inhabitants, who have lived with their customs and economic and political models.

The holistic economic model never and in no form should be imposed forcefully on a person or a nation, as this was conducted with capitalism during the colonization of lands. The disappointment of the principles on which are based the capitalistic societies and the search for better working solutions of present day global challenges, will provide the opportunity for the holistic paradigm to find its followers, ideological keepers and political pioneers in societies. One of the most important fields, which require transformation of the relationships in the society, is the economy in all aspects, related to it.

Unlike the capitalistic and communistic systems, the holistic initiates the economic processes by firstly gathering the need of every participant of the organization and then making an assessment. The production with resources which are public property is complied with the interests of the subjects of the holistic model. Therefore, this is an economy, which is built to transform the resources into goods in such a way, which would bring the best satisfaction of the interests of the subjects of the holistic model, for a particular historic time. Holistic economy is the process of creating, offering, distributing, using and recycling of goods in a way which protects the interests of humankind, animals, plants and Earth. This is a significant distinction with the capitalistic economy, which relies on meeting the demand and supply by colliding private interests of many actors, without being relevant the interests of the biological species and the planet.

Capitalistic system considers all its participants (including humans) as a replaceable resource, which can be used by a dominating legal subject on his discretion, regardless of the joyful development of all living organisms. Holistic economy differs substantially from capitalistic also in its principles of distribution of goods, produced with public resources.

Their provision is conducted with priority of classes of needs for all participants of the organization, as this is seen as a human right which the system has to protect.

In this way the holistic economy arranges into classes the needs and not the people, as this is conducted in capitalism. Labor process in turn is function of implementation of this human right and of directly organized satisfaction of the needs of the participants.

1. The principle of equal rights to public goods

It is necessary to be thickly highlighted that the holistic model does not foresee depriving or forcibly expropriating private property. The holistic organization does not forbid private property as a legal institute, because this would mean huge violation of rights and freedoms of the people and introducing dictatorship in the name of equality ones again! Even more, inviolability of private property is protected in much greater extend for a private person in a state, which has adopted the holistic model. The first example, which proves this statement, is that a holistic state would not sanction a criminal behavior by forcibly expropriating private property of the person, who has committed a crime. Secondly, if private property is needed for public goods, it would not be possible to be forcibly expropriated and substituted with an equivalent property of the state, as it is a common practice in capitalistic societies.

In modern legal systems always exists the possibility private property to be expropriated by the state on the grounds of public needs as well as a form of sanction for criminal activities. These legal possibilities are not put in the focus of attention to the people in capitalistic societies, who are persuaded by official that private property is sacrosanct for the state. In fact it is not.

Main specific of the holistic economy is that public resources are managed as a unified organism and are used for creation of goods and services, which are freely accessible for the participants and distributed relatively equally in quality and quantity between them. This system aims to satisfy the classes of needs to the participants and to be flexible for their individual preferences.

The production and distribution of goods from part of the public resources, owned by the holistic organization, and the provision of free and equal access to goods and services, is of key importance for the creation of holistic society.

As was written above, the distribution should not refer to all public property, because some of it is needed for the people who are conducting specific activities, for example a cosmonaut and his space suit or a fireman and his fire suit and technical equipment. In the beginning these types of goods should not be set for equal access and free distribution upon a request. In case of good governance of the holistic organization there will be included more and more public goods and services with free access.

On the capitalistic motto "There is no thing as free lunch" is presented the holistic alternative one: "The lunch is free, when we are creating it together and sharing between each other."

Why equal access to goods and services, created with public resources is important?

Firstly, this is direct and practical application of the fundamental principle and value that all people are equally important manifestations of the humankind and of the Absolute and therefore deserve equal access to goods and services, particularly to those, created with public resources. Equal access to goods and services is validation of their equal opportunity to develop themselves in the service to the whole. If is provided the opportunity a person to receive his needed products as well as all other participants of the holistic organization, gradually will be eliminated the class division of society, based on economic criteria. This would be a huge step towards elimination of the notion that one group of people deserves more rights than another.

For the holistic organization the primary function of the goods and services is to support the people in pursue of happiness and in their creative impulses to improve the life of all. Goods and services are not used as a reward in the holistic organization and their deprivation is never used as a form of sanction to a person, or an organization.

The right to receive for free a product, created from public resources, at the same time with every other participant is the relevant criteria to achieve equality in distribution of goods and services. For example, if a person doesn't want to eat strawberries in a particular day, he is not going to order a delivery of strawberries. However, the possibility these fruits to be delivered to him, if he desires, is what put him equally in distribution of goods with all other participants. This principle is much more appreciative to the individuality and freedom of the person to choose whether to use or not a specific product, instead of giving everyone the same type of goods, without regards of their preferences. Therefore, maintaining equal access to public goods is important to sustain equal economic rights in a holistic organization. In order to be fulfilled the principle of equal access to goods the inclusion of every product for distribution to the participants should be when it is in the need quantity to satisfy the needs of those participants, who desire to order it.

Through introducing equal access to public goods and service the organization aims to stimulate the people to be more focused on what they are giving with their work to the organization, instead of thinking what they could afford to buy with their salary, as it is in egoistic systems. What a person receives in a holistic organization is an indicator whether it is managed well and whether the participants are capable to achieve the desired results. The abundance for every participant would become a reality, if the management utilizes the resources and governs well and the motivation of the participants is high.

The equal access refers to the products, which are public property of the holistic organization and not to the private property of its participants.

Holistic organization can be also a private corporation, which aims to transform itself, according to the holistic model. In this hypothesis it has to organize the management and redistribution of significant part of its property between its participants in a way which protects the interests of the subjects of the holistic model. There is no difference whether the property is of private or public and whether the organization is a corporation, a state, or an international organization as long as it is governed in the interest of the whole and equal access is provided to all participants.

The distribution in the holistic organization refers only to its members and not to all people. This limitation is necessary for many reasons. The first reason is that the resources of the organization are assigned to be used holistically by people, who are sharing the vision of holistic society. Participants are going to be motivated to work and to create, if they are sure that the products of the organization would be used with respect to the values of the community. This principle will strengthen the resilience, stability and self-sufficiency of the organization. Every other person, who is willing to receive products by a holistic organization, should have signed an agreement for cooperation with it, or to be in the process of becoming its member.

The access to goods and services for the participants of the holistic organization replaces the different payment in currency for their labor, devaluation and overvaluation of the products and the creation of different economic access for different working positions. In the process of elimination of the intermediaries in the internal trading, the over-pricing of these products will decrease drastically, which means using much less resources of human labor to introduce a product in circulation to reach its final customer, who have ordered it.

It should be noted that modern day lack in economy is to large extend related to low remuneration and to overpricing of the products until they reach the market. Elimination of overpricing and of differentiation in the access to public goods and services will result in much more products for every participant.

In capitalistic society, equal access to goods in understood as the opportunity for everyone to buy a product on the free market, if he has the asked financial resources for it. Economic stratification and different remuneration of the people leads to a situation when a luxury product is too expensive for most of them and it becomes inaccessible. Even basic goods are impossible to be bought from many people, because their labor is evaluated as low. A product which is offered in the free market is available only for those, who can pay the price, the merchant wants for it.

The system of service to the whole does not use the provision of goods as a desired motivation for starting a job, or getting involved with a project. In the holistic organization the goods and services, which are created from public resources have the purpose to satisfy the needs of the participants by being managed in the best interest of the subjects of the holistic model.

Transparency of the system, strengthening of the motivation to live in service to the whole and expert criteria for reaching high-level managing positions are serious prerequisites for good governance.

How a human right does emerge and why most of the societies start to observe it?

The only reason a human right to emerge is when critical mass of people starts to express confidently their will that they desire respectful and human treatment towards themselves, or towards a group of beings in specific aspect of their relationship with others. The accepted human right not only delimitate the boundaries of the actions of the state towards the particular group, but presents a due care towards this group of people, or other beings. In this way society is restructured significantly and harmonious attitudes and respectful behavior are legally regulated.

Modern day societies have not reached the level of recognizing and accepting all human rights and this means they prefer to maintain an order of inhumane attitudes, relationship and social division.

In the system of service to the whole large amounts of the public goods are distributed, without being necessary to be sold to the participants, as explained above. A lot of energy and resources would be saved, because of avoiding competition and because of creating a system, which serves the man and other beings and not vise-versa.

Modern capitalistic model is building social relationships by purposefully creating shortages and economic holes, which are used to cripple the development of ordinary individuals and whole nations. Problems are created in order to find temporary solutions. The result is services which can be afforded by one group of people and remain unaffordable for another. The division of society on the basis of the goods, they own, polarizes poor and rich people. Both groups are fighting for their survival and are encouraged to live in service to the self.

There are several leading academic models of the American capitalistic class society, which is considered as a modern example for all nations of creating of social system in service to the self. They are very close to each other and the definitions and the numbers, they are presenting. Below are shown three of the most popular models. The first one is presented by Dennis Gilbert [16] and published in 2002; the second - by Leonard Beeghley [17] in 2004 and the third - by William Thompson and Joseph Hickey [18] in 2005.

---

16 Gilbert, D. (2002). *The American Class Structure: In An Age of Growing Inequality.* Belmont, CA: Wadsworth

17 Beeghley, L. (2004). *The Structure of Social Stratification in the United States.* Boston, MA: Pearson, Allyn & Bacon

18 Thompson, W. & Hickey, J. (2005). *Society in Focus.* Boston, MA: Pearson, Allyn & Bacon

Social stratification models

Table

Dennis Gilbert		Leonard Beeghley		William Thompson & Joseph Hickey	
Class	Typical Characteristics	Class	Typical Characteristics	Class	Typical Characteristics
Capitalist (1%)	Top-level executives, high-rung politicians, heirs. Ivy League education common.	Super rich (0.9%)	Multi-millionaires whose incomes commonly exceed $350.000; includes celebrities and powerful executives/ politicians. Ivy League education common.	Upper (1%)	Top-level executives, celebrities, heirs; income of $500.000+ is common. Ivy League education common.
Upper middle class (15%)	Highly-educated (often with graduate degrees), most commonly salaried, proffesionals and middle management with large work autonomy.	The rich (5%)	Households with net worth of $1 million or more; largely in the form of home equity. Generally have college degrees.	Upper middle class (15%)	Highly-educated (often with graduate degrees) professionals & managers with household incomes varying from the high 5-figure range to commonly above $100.000.
Lower middle class (30%)	Semi-professionals and craftsmen with a roughly average standard of living. Most have some college education and are white-collar.	Middle class (46%)	College-educated workers with considerably higher-than-average incomes and compensations; a man making $57.000 and a woman making $40.000 may be typical.	Lower middle class (32%)	Semi-professionals and craftsmen with some work autonomy; household incomes commonly range from $35.000 to $75.000. Typically, some college education.
Working class (30%)	Clerical and most blue-collar workers whose work is routinized. Standard of living varies depending on number of income earners, but is commonly just adequate. High school education.	Working class (40 - 45%)	Blue-collar workers and those whose jobs are highly routinized with low economic security; a man making $40.000 and a woman making $26.000 may be typical. High school education.	Working class (32%)	Clerical, pink- and blue-collar workers with often low job security; common household incomes range from $16.000 to $30.000. High school education.
Working poor (13%)	Service, low-rung clerical and some blue-collar workers. High economic insecurity and risk of poverty. Some high school education.	The poor (12%)	Those living below the poverty line with limited to no participation in the labor force; a household income of $18.000 may be typical. Some high school education.	Lower class (14 - 20%)	Those who occupy poorly-paid positions or rely on government transfers. Some high school education.
Underclass (12%)	Those with limited or no participation in the labor force. Reliant on government transfers. Some high school education.				

The main conclusions which we can reach from reviewing these models are that in modern egoistic economic systems of social stratification there are two main criteria for determining the social group of a person.

The first is quantitative and is related to the property of the person and the income that he receives.

The second criterion is qualitative and is related with the status, that a person is given in the society. Beside his financial wealth this status can be awarded on the grounds of ancestral affiliation, achievements in certain field or an ordinary fame, which is not related with any special qualities.

Most of the people have been brought up with the attitude that social stratification on the grounds of economic division is a normal form of social order. For them it would seem unjust to be provided equal access to public goods, which are given to the participants as an act of economic right and not as a form of direct payment. The reason for this sensation of injustice lays in the persuasion of the masses that goods are supposed to be distributed unequally in order to serve as an indicator for personal achievements and public importance. In the public opinion is formed the thesis that "some people are better than others", "more responsible", "contribute more to society" and therefore they "deserve" bigger access to goods than others. Of course people, who are relying just on the public opinion are incapable to provide a meaningful answer to the question: Is it fair an honest person to work decently on three job positions, in order to provide the minimum for his family? They would ascribe this phenomenon to small disadvantage of the system and the lack of good education for the person, but they would not be able to find a theoretical solution to this systematic problem. Such thinking is intrinsic to people, who continue to regard goods as stimulus, which means thinking in the framework of an egoistic system.

The holistic organization manages and distributes its public property and it is its right and duty to stipulate the principle for equal access to public goods as a manifestation of basic human right. As the right to live is basic human right, which is not disputed by most states, as the right of equal access to public goods should become for the holistic organizations.

The stability of the capitalistic system is to large extend due to the circumstance that people are playing the social roles, that the system foresees for them and are unable to form a new model in the service to the whole, with more harmonious social roles. This means that the capitalist accumulates and protects his wealth and is looking for a way to make bigger profit only because his employees are unable to find another way of living and are enticed to be part of this plan as voiceless figures, who are not demanding service to the whole. If a person does not like the social role of an employee of a certain organization, in capitalistic system for him exists the opportunity to change it, or to become a salesman, or to provide some form of service, through which he could try to change the social role he is playing in society. Despite this personal change of the separate individual and the fact that he finds another job, this does not result in improving of the capitalistic system. The reason is that the effect of the labor does not necessarily leads to better satisfaction of the interests of humankind and the whole, if a person is forced by the market to exploit humans, animals, plants and Earth in order to remain competitive and make a profit. This merchant would be bounded to supply only the products that people are demanding.

The holistic model is presented as an alternative of the capitalistic one, and not as creation of a new social role or humanization of already existing in the frame of the capitalistic system. It is because of the different aims, placed in the systems, different approaches and methods that are used in them.

How would function the economy of a society, when is stimulated the driving force of service to the whole?

The responsible attitude towards the natural resources and their balanced use in the manufacturing process and consumption are of primal importance for preserving them for the future generations of humankind. This is main priority of the holistic economy. From the viewpoint of humankind Earth should be regarded as a superior being, which has accommodated many life forms, including humans. This vision guides us towards care for the planet for its own good and resource management which does not violate drastically its energetic balance. Therefore, the interest of humankind should never contradict the interest of Earth. On this principle is based the holistic economy - from production, logistics, consumption to recycling. It is necessary to be conducted many multidisciplinary researches in order to determine the right methods and technologies to perform all the processes. One of the most important principles should be the use of renewable energetic sources and technologies which are nature friendly in every stage of the economic processes. Their application should be widened to the point of becoming the only sources of energy. Finding the balance in the production process includes also nurturing animals and plants not only as a human resource, but caring for them as beings in a gentle ecological environment. The need to consume some of the species is undisputed at this point of human development, but it is very important to implement the principle of minimum violation of their interests in performing all human activities.

The development of technologies and wide introduction of renewable energetic sources in capitalistic society would not lead to cardinal social change in the states and to improvement of the life of the majority of people. Such technologies might be friendly to Earth, but they would still remain an economic burden for people, because capitalism requires constant dependence and carefully managed exploitation of everyone. People would never receive something, if they do not pay for it in egoistic system. Even when the energy comes from the Sun, for the ownership of needed devices a tax would be introduced, or they would be designed to be too expensive or for short-term usage, so that dependence is maintained and people are not free.

The conclusion is that introduction of new technologies in the civilization today would be positive for the humankind only if social changes are following them. Without such transformation of the social model, humans would remain economic slaves in an inhumane caste system.

Another basic principle in the holistic economy is that the products should be durable, maximum time of use and easily upgraded. Presently, many of the corporations are stimulated to develop non-durable products, to use materials with low quality and not the optimal technologies, which are available in order to be competitive for decades ahead and to provide cheap and new products as planned. Products with high quality which are durable are more expensive for most customers and less profitable for business, because the customers will not return for the new product next year.

Every reader is capable of finding many items, which were durable decades ago unlike their counterparts today. Behind this change relies economic logic and businesses are not supposed to be blamed for following it, because the market requires it. This economic logic is unfavorable and sometimes harmful for the users and it leads to negative impact on natural resources of Earth and unnecessary prolonging of retention of people in the production stage of economy. Typical examples of such products are automobiles and mobile devices. Contemporary capitalism and particularly the global market are forcing corporations to introduce innovation with a much slower step and with many new products in order to maximize the profits of their shareholders for generations. In the holistic economic model this compromise with innovations and useful life of items not only is unnecessary, but it is extremely undesirable, because much more natural resources and human resources are used in order to satisfy the same needs.

Holistic production includes the most ecological way of manufacturing of every product in a quality, which is optimal in matter of functions and as much possible to endure.

The implementation of these conditions would lead to much less use of natural resources with technologies which are much favorable to Earth.

The next advantage is that in all economic processes will be used much less human labor, because technological optimization would not lead to deprivation of basic goods for people, because products will be much durable and much easier for upgrade. In order to achieve these positive results, the economic activities should be planned presciently in an unseen scale until now and by completely different criteria than bigger profit for corporations.

The holistic organization has the authority to determine what type of goods should be produced and what kind of services provided with public resources, in order to be satisfied the interest of the whole and to be fulfilled in the best possible way the needs and desires of the participants of the organization. The selection of these items is made after gathering the preferences of all participants. At first glance this approach may seem limited and contradictory of the principles of the free market, but it is not correct and below is explained why.

What are the principles on which basis is produced one item in the capitalistic system? The cornerstone is whether there will be demand

and who is capable to afford it and keep buying this type of products from the same corporation in the future. This leads to distortions and vicious practices in the relationship between a merchant and a customer. It is well known that good merchants are succeeding in influencing the desires of customers to acquire certain good. Modern marketing and maintained attitudes for social status impact the people significantly and shapes their culture of increasing consumerism and desire to have more and luxury goods.

The holistic economic model changes the prism and focuses on determining the real natural need of the consumer and to classify them by priority. It is an individually oriented economic model which satisfies the needs of the people at the same level and at the same time. The goods and services are produced, following the above mentioned principles of ecology, durability and optimal technical functionality.

Logically, determining the needs includes regarding the preferences of all participants and estimating the potential of the holistic organization to satisfy them. If the organization is unable to provide specific good, because it is from a higher class, too luxurious, or does not correspond with the interest of the whole, the person is free to acquire it on the free market as it happens in capitalistic societies today. The holistic system does not enforce more rigid regime of limitations than capitalism, but through good governance of the public resources it creates much bigger opportunities and much larger access to high quality of goods and services.

For example a member of the holistic organization may desire to have his own uniquely made 20-meter long yacht with public resources. The employees, who are responsible for applying the algorithm of evaluation of the needs of the holistic community and drawing out the priorities for satisfaction, would determine easily that it is not justified to use public resources for the creation of this type of items for everyone, who desire them, because they are very high class products. Therefore this product would not be in circulation for order and would not be provided to the person, because this would violate the principle of equal access to goods, produced with public resources. In this case the person, who desires to own such a yacht, is free to acquire it by paying someone to build it by paying him with his private property. This illustrates the distinction of the holistic system from the communistic, in which such an opportunity for free entrepreneurship is forbidden and luxurious goods and services are preserved for the high echelon of the communistic party.

Diversity of provided goods

Production of goods with public resources, intended for all participants of the holistic organization, does not mean that people would have the same things. On the contrary, the holistic system will be able to adopt itself to the individual needs and desires of the people to much larger extent than the capitalistic state, because the goods in the system are made on individual demand. How many people are ordering individual design of their house, or of their automobile, or of their clothes in capitalistic society? A few have such economic privilege and very few people have the esthetic desire for individual creative self-expression instead of blind following of tendencies and fashion.

In good governance and following the principles of the holistic society, every participant would have the opportunity to make an individual choice in the optimal boundaries of the system and not depending on his financial resources. Every holistic organization is going to have different capabilities and will draw different confines, but the participants will surely receive much more qualitative goods and services, which will be created on demand individually for him.

It would become achieved for every participant, without being necessary for him to pay, but because of the application of the mutual agreement between the person and the organization to provide desired labor in the service to the community. The subject of labor relations is separately studied in chapter six.

Presently, the cost of every product includes the expenses for the materials that it is made of, marketing, advertisement, logistics, petroleum footprint, costs for remuneration of the employees, profit for the manufacturer and profit for all merchants on the chain of intermediaries and many other components. The result is huge overpricing of every product and attachment of parasite components, which are not adding value to the good. When is increased the value of a good or service, this means that the person should find a way to increase his financial resources. The legal possibility for achieving such an increase is to work more.

The aim of the capitalistic market is to take the money of the person and his need is just a means for luring him. In the holistic system the creation of an item with public resources is conducted with the clear aim to satisfy the need of a participant. The focus of the system is on the useful effect of the product for the consumer. This would lead to huge optimization of the production process and to the removing of unnecessarily overpricing economic components on the chain. For example it would be unjustified to advertise an item which is foreseen to be provided for free to the person. This means that all costs for this activity and all human energy towards it would be redirected and substituted with ordinary information of the participants that the item is available and what are its characteristics. The function of the advertisement to influence the desires of the people and to form his intention to acquire certain good or service are undesirable for the holistic system, because it is important that products are satisfying needs which people are aware of and which are useful for him. The fact that advertisements are often forming artificial desires and attitudes among certain target group of consumers is a problem for the holistic economy, because it overshadows the freedom of the individual to evaluate calmly what are his needs.

The holistic system needs to have intelligent consumers, who understand in-depth not only their needs, but also the need of all participants and all people, because political decisions would be based on the understandings of all participants. These are consumers with high ethical standards which are based on self-respect, but also on respect of other people's needs. In order to have such consumers, the education and information campaigns for the people should be encouraging the emergence of free, intelligent and good-hearted people. Only then consumers would be able to reach high level of personal awareness and self-responsibility. They would be able to make a distinction between their real natural needs from selfish egoistic desires, which are manipulated by outer forces. Such a consumer is not going to encourage himself to be dependent on a particular unhealthy product or to develop too much dependence to an ordinary product or service.

The holistic system should not include in the access to free goods and services products for which is scientifically proven that are unhealthy. It should not be encouraged excessive dependence to certain goods, because it is not in the interest of the individual and therefore not in the interest of the whole humankind. If a product is legally allowed to be on the market, even though it is proven to be unhealthy, it should be accessible to be bought and not provided for free. An example of such product is cigarettes. In this case the free will of the people is regarded and they can have access to these items. At the same time the holistic organization does not endorse addiction to unhealthy products and does not allocate resources for their production.

Capitalistic system, unlike the holistic one, needs to have easily amenable consumers, who can become dependent on different products and who can be manipulated via marketing tricks. This situation is favorable for businesses and for income of states. The prerequisite to create dependencies of the consumers leads to significant distortions in the whole economic process which is hindering the harmonic development of the individual and is not in the interest of the whole.

This need of easily amenable and irrational people is a huge obstacle for educational systems and instead of upbringing people with critical thinking, creative and responsible, capitalism is growing sheep, shepherds and wolves. Self-control, healthy decency and measure are highly unwanted features in people's ethical system, because this will decrease the role of marketing, it would lead to less sales of products and overall constriction of economy. Much profitable for business is to pray on the unbalanced attitudes and addictions of the people instead of being of service to their development with the goods they are producing.

Completely different relation to things is presented in the holistic society. Therefore completely different purpose has the holistic economy.

The global planning of the whole economic process in a holistic organization leads to eliminating competition among its participants. However, competition will remain between it and the capitalistically oriented subjects, including states, corporations and individuals. Consequently, in the early stages of application of the holistic economy will be outlined the following tendency: the basic economic needs will be satisfied by the holistic organization and secondary, unhealthy and luxurious goods will be provided by capitalistic subjects for certain payment or barter. In case of good governance the holistic organization would become capable to provide secondary goods, which do not harm people's health.

Global management of public resources in the interest of the whole will lead to decreasing the pressure over the production to make more and more goods and to widen the scope of consumers. It will be substituted by a stimulus for best possible governance and satisfaction of real natural need of the whole community by producing useful goods on demand. This motivation for the employees in the holistic economy will lead to much more creative solutions and much bigger level of satisfaction to all participants than capitalism is capable to propose.

2. Classes of needs instead classes of people

Satisfying the interest of humankind requires to be made a detailed estimate of the needs of the participants in the holistic organization. The matching of individual preferences of all participants with the optimal capabilities of the holistic organization includes the right of the person to choose what to consume, in what quantities and how often to change the object with a new one. As was already mentioned above the holistic system foresees freedom of entrepreneurship and private initiative and allows everyone to pursue satisfaction of their desires, if this is not bringing harm to the person or to others and is legally allowed. It can be achieved by commercial activities in the same way as it is done in capitalistic societies. The essential difference is that a large part of the public resources is going to be managed and allocated in a way to achieve equal access to goods and services for all participants in a step-wise character of satisfying separate classes of needs.

The classes of needs define which needs and desires are with a priority over others. This classification is necessary for satisfying the interests of the community, because through it can be achieved prioritization of the use of resources and their distribution to guarantee equal access to goods and services. It is of primal importance for good governance of human labor, which is provided by the participants in service to the whole. The result is that the labor process in holistic economy is directed to answer directly to the needs of the individuals and the community of the present moment. The same cannot be stated for the capitalistic system in which private corporations are the main employers and they are choosing the direction of labor for their employees by the criteria to profit from a specific demand, not necessarily a public need. Private corporations are trying to survive in a harsh competitive environment and human labor is their means, without trying to develop society in the best possible way.

Classification of the needs requires separate and thorough research, which comprises all types of needs, which the holistic organization should be responsible to satisfy. This classification is a reflection of the understanding that the society has about human-beings. The precise prioritization would determine the types of goods and services which would be distributed for every participant.

It is important to clarify that differentiating the needs on classes does not regard art, entertainments, tourism, science, sports or other undoubtedly important activities as less significant than the provision of home, food and water. Differentiation is made in relation to priorities of the conditions for living and not with the aim to evaluate which economic branch is more important than other. Classes of needs can be defined as different elements of a house, where basic needs represent its walls, ground floor and roof, whereas higher class needs are symbolizes its painting and furnishing.

Before starting to distribute public goods and services by class, it is necessary to decide which products the holistic organization would provide for free, which would be on the free market for trade with external parties and which would be forbidden for trade. Such an assessment of the regime of commercial goods is conducted today too in capitalistic societies, where some products are sold without restrictions for the buyers, some require special approval and others are forbidden for all. In capitalistic society there aren't clearly defined criteria what products to be available on the free market. In most cases, if there is a demand, there would be a supply and for the state it is more profitable, if it is legally regulated. The social impact of products and the effect they are causing to the health of people is of secondary importance, if there is a strong demand for them. The same example with cigarettes can be pointed out, because they are causing damages for health and at the same time are creating addiction. Another example for the lack of criteria is the liberal regime of buying automatic guns in many states, which are considered as developed. If a person has to defend himself with automatic weapons in his home and in his town, this means that the state is not having good policies in many fields and society is in very low level of development.

The holistic system, unlike the capitalistic one, is caring for the health and positive social development of its participants. It creates much more opportunities for freedom of expression and satisfies directly the economic rights for all people, but only if the products are healthy and cannot easily bring harm to society.

As this is performed presently, every particular product would have to be reviewed by an expert commission, but the criteria would be to serve the consumers and the whole in the best possible way. It would not be legal to lobby for distribution of low quality and dangerous products, because someone could profit from them. If the holistic organization is governed well, the results would be free provision of much more useful goods and services, than are sold in the most developed capitalistic states for their middle classes.

The second aspect of forming responsible consumer demand is related with education and information campaigns. In capitalistic systems it is visible that if such activities are organized well, they have enormous positive impact to limit unhealthy dependencies. The mere fact that capitalistic states consider letting go unhealthy and dangerous products to the market is presenting the inhumane face of egoistic economy.

In the holistic system after determining which goods are useful and can be included for free and equal distribution, they should be prioritized in the corresponding class of needs in the holistic organization.

The classification of the needs is not connected with the capabilities of the holistic organization to satisfy them in a particular moment. For example, if there is poor management in a holistic organization and it cannot provide diversity of healthy food for the people, it does not change the fact that they need healthy food.

The main principle for achieving equality in distribution of public goods is that first class (basic) needs are satisfied firstly and for every participant. After everyone in the holistic organization can exercise his right to order and receive goods and services from first class, the organization is eligible to move on the next stage of satisfying needs from higher class. Needs from second class are those which are not directly required for the survival of the individual, but they are an absolute necessity for his ethical, cultural, scientific and spiritual development and from improvement of his ways of self-expression in life.

After describing and classifying the needs, the holistic organization has to regulate the access to which goods and services would lead to their satisfaction. Among the basic needs of all participants it is fair to place their feeding and healthy food as the good which can satisfy this need. What would be the food, that the person is going to consume will decide himself of course. The holistic system will have to provide the opportunity for much larger variety of useful products for every participant, which is not possible for capitalistic and communistic societies. The reason for this is because only in the holistic society the human labor and the other resources will be directed towards achieving this variety and selfish desire for profit would not hinder the production of goods, as it the case in egoistic systems. The production of low quality, unhealthy and even dangerous food, with the aim to reduce costs would become bygone - bad habit, intrinsic for capitalistic food industry.

The aim of the holistic economy is to satisfy the individual needs of all participants and this is what distinguishes it significantly from capitalistic and communistic ones. The last two limit access to the goods and services for most of the people in order to provide the highest quality of products to a minority of the privileged. To achieve satisfaction of the needs of the participants of the holistic organization it has to be conducted simultaneously for everyone as regards to one class of needs.

If we accept that entertainments fall into second and higher class of needs, because they are not directly related to the immediate survival of the individual, it is fair to initiate their satisfaction after guaranteeing that the lower class of needs of all participants are met. This principle guarantees the humane, harmonious and balanced development of the community and implements in practice the value that every human-being is equally important individual manifestation of the whole humankind.

The equal access to public goods will gradually lead to elimination of the economic social stratification. The subjective estimate that one job position deserves more or less goods and services than others will not be applied. In modern days many people do not want to be part of such society in which economic status is not used for diversification. Those people are programmed to think that classes of people are natural phenomenon for society and this is the "normal" way to establish a working order. Even more belonging to a specific economic class have become basic fundament for psychological developing of the personality. Capitalism requires from people to think themselves mainly from the perspective of their social class, because in this way is maintained division among people. Division of people is the cornerstone for ruling people in the prisons of egoistic societies.

Despite the fact that one job position requires more knowledge and skills than another, the access to goods and services should not be changed and to be used as an incentive for the participants and stimulus for applying for a job in the holistic organization. The desire and the abilities of a person to be useful to others and to the whole with the performance of a specific labor is the main stimulus, which is encouraged in the working process in the holistic society. Economic privileges, granting larger access to goods and services for a particular job position or for a particular group of people are a gross violation of the principles of building a holistic organization. Norms and actions, which are causing this type of division and social conflict, would be considered as a form of corruption and violation of the ideals of the holistic society. People, who would conduct such actions or who are trying to implement such policies, are demonstrating their lack of understanding of the grounding principles of the holistic system. When there isn't understanding of these principles, the person should not be able to grow in his career development in the holistic organization, because his actions and general approach for personal motivation and encouragement of other colleagues would be contradictory to the principle of economic equality of all participants and the driving force of service to the whole.

Good example of the absence of division, based on economic reward for people, who possess different skills and knowledge, we can find today in the loving family. A good parent does not provide healthy and more expensive food for the child, who is bringing home better grades in school, than the other, who did not cope so well. The food in such families is distributed by taste and not by merit. Goods and services in loving families are not used as a reward, but as a form of expressing family care for the development and joy of the particular member.

The next fundamental difference between the egoistic and holistic models is visible in the attitude towards the participants and particularly whether the organizations are considering them consequently as dependable resources, or as unique and indispensible manifestation of the Absolute. This distinction marks the completely different purposes of existing of both systems. In the first type the organizations are exploiting the participants and sucking their energy in order to feed the higher echelon, while the second facilitates the relationships between them and manages and distributes the energy in the interest of everyone.

The holistic model is considering, preserving and developing the unique features of the participants in a holistic organization. The freedom of everyone to determine his own path of personal development is a value for the person and for the holistic community. The purpose of the holistic organization is to support this free choice to be in the service to the whole, because this would lead to the most beneficial results for everyone.

Capitalistic model perceives all participants by the prism of the social class in which they are. The personal achievements are valued (including in money) by the abilities of the subject to procure different type of energy and to direct public opinion. Regarding humans as replaceable resource for the economy leads to significant problems for human survival, but also blocks the sensation of the people that they are spiritual entities with a higher purpose, who are manifestation of the whole Absolute.

The capitalistic system builds and maintains extremely limited vision of the human-being. If the person accepts it, he is doomed to create unhappiness for himself and others around him.

When we review the uniqueness of every participant in a holistic organization, this means that we adapt the whole system towards his needs to the level in which this is optimal for the organization. If the organization is governed well, the result would be better and more comprehensive adaptation of the system to the participants. It can be achieved in all stages of the economic process and for all products. For example it can be present in the individual architecture and design of the house, automobile, design of the clothes, variety of healthy food, quality entertainments and reaches flexibility of the working time, personal satisfaction of the labor etc.

What individual freedom provides the capitalistic model?

Modern day capitalism has transformed itself significantly, so that it can offer more freedom for its participants, comparing to what they used to have in the past centuries. This positive result is achieved because of the claiming of basic human rights, among which is the partial removal of racial and gender inequality in all states. The second prerequisite of achieving more freedom is related to technological development. The last can easily become a tool for complete dictatorship and lack of personal space. The exercising of this freedom has its cost metaphorically and literally. It is necessary for the person to have money, which means to have acquired social energy in order to exercise his right to buy desired goods and services. The aim of the seller almost never is to satisfy in the best way the need of the buyer, but it is to take as much money as possible from him and to create a psychological bond of dependence between the product and the customer. The seller concentrates his energy to develop this bond and to exploit it in the future, in order to guarantee his own survival and prosperity.

One of the most profitable world corporations, for which every reader can guess, are making huge profits from products, which are harmful for health of the people or are not objects of primal necessity in the system of class of needs. Their marketing strategies are successful and they are capable to make even the harmful product to become an object of desire. This way of economic functioning is in violation of the interest of the whole and deforms the social relationships. Logically, the holistic economic system should not use public resources for stimulating the emergence of harmful products.

Modern day capitalism is organized globally and the inequality of the people is not visible only inside a state, but it is still maintained between races of people. The thesis that colonialism has been dismantled is partially true and we should not forget that the population of many developing countries cannot free itself from despotic regimes and inhumane practices. These rulers are quietly, but stably supported by western governments and other leading nations. In order to illustrate the truthfulness of this statement let's make a brief review of the manufacturing and commercial cycles of a product, which is used predominantly by western societies - the cocoa.

As main substance of all chocolate products, the manufacturing of cocoa is crucial for the whole chocolate economic branch, which is making income from sales around $100 billion per year.[19] The consumption of chocolate products is predominant in European countries and in the United States and it is more than 70% than the total world consumption.[20] Approximately the same percentage, or about 2/3 of the total cocoa, is produced in only two countries - Cote d'Ivoire and Ghana.[21] Therefore there is solid and visible interdependency between the economics of these two countries and the consumption in the western nations. For years there are hard evidences of massive exploitation of children as "slave labors" in the production of cocoa in these countries.[22] Not every child labor is considered "slave", but when there is continuation of 12 hours/day for minors, prohibition for education, unsafe usage of chemicals, very low remuneration, than these are very serious violations of several international legal norms. Detailed study on the topic of slave child labor in Western Africa concludes that more than 2.03 million children are conducting dangerous labor in the manufacturing of cocoa in Cote d'Ivoire and Ghana.[23] If western corporations which are buying cocoa from them had not information about these atrocities, they should have made more research, before buying the products. There is clear double standard in treating human-beings from different races and this is harsh violation of the interests of humankind. Evidence that western corporations not only accept the status quo in the production of cocoa, but they are trying to maintain it, is visible in the efforts of US lobbyists to block an international agreement aimed at ending the worst forms of child labor, known as Harkin–Engel Protocol.[24] Even that revised version of the protocol is finally adopted, the measures, which are applied, do not lead to significant diminishing of the problem.

---

19 Global Chocolate, Cocoa Beans, Lecithin, Sugar and Vanilla Market (2011-2016), www.marketsandmarkets.com/PressReleases/global-chocolate-market.asp

20 www.statista.com/topics/1638/chocolate-industry/

21 Data from International Cocoa Organization, http://www.icco.org/economy/production.html

22 www.foodispower.org/slavery-chocolate/

23 Final report of Tulane University, *Survey Research on Child Labor in West African Cocoa Growing Areas*, 2015

24 Harkin–Engel Protocol www.childlabor-payson.org/meetings/

The conclusion which we can make is that the low cost of the cocoa remains top priority for western corporations and their governments and all forms of violation of human rights, including those of children, are acceptable in the name of larger profit. The capitalistic system continues to maintain unawareness and indifference among the consumers, in order to manage the economic processes and stimulate high consumption easily.

Unlike capitalism, the holistic system cannot tolerate exploitation of children or other form of inhumane exploitation of its participants or external persons. The reason is because holistic organization does not aim accumulation of capital and does not stimulate an abyss of greed among people, which is filled with the deprivation of others and often with their inhumane monstrous treatment.

Every participant has its dignified place in the holistic organization which gives him the opportunity to serve in the best possible way to the whole. It is his right to find it, to shape it and to become one with it. The role of the community is to assist him to unfold his highest and most beautiful potential, as this would be in his best interest and also of the whole.

3. Holistic production

The organization of the manufacturing process in a holistic economy requires excellent knowledge of the interests of humankind, animals, plants and Earth, because it aims to satisfy them in the best possible way. This means that before certain product is manufactured, distributed, used and recycled, it is absolutely necessary to be made estimations how all planned activities would affect these four interests.

Capitalistic system on the other hand does not aim to satisfy the interests of these subjects, including those of humankind. It is completely enough to look at how Earth, plants or animals are used and whether the created products are equally accessible to all people on the planet.

The main purpose of the holistic economy is to facilitate the satisfaction of the interest of the whole. This means that a balance should be found between abundance and sufficiency. Elimination of overconsumption and building of more and more harmonious relationships between the subjects of the holistic model is another objective of the holistic economy.

Regarding plants and animals as commodities, which are necessary source of energy for human-beings is inevitable, but the holistic approach foresees to think of them firstly as other manifestations of the Absolute, which deserve good life. Our interaction with them should be respectful as to living beings and only after that as to a resource, if necessary. In the consideration of the interests of other biological species it is important to take into account the amount of goods, which are produced and those which are substituted on their place.

In the holistic economy optimal production is not the one which is capable to bring profit. It is not the one which can be consumed in the biggest possible quantities. Optimal production is a combination of ecological obtaining of goods, avoidance of overproduction or scarcity, creation of high quality products by humanely usage of labor, balanced consumption of the participants and equal access to goods for everyone.

In order to achieve such production, it is necessary to conduct large scale research of the needs of the members of the holistic organization. It should be followed by planning of the whole economic process, so that enough goods are created, overproduction is prevented and depletion of the corresponding resources is avoided.

Another huge difference with capitalistic system is that the holistic does not rely on free market initiative to satisfy the needs of the people, but does not forbid it, as it happened in communistic regimes. The reasons are plain and simple: the entrepreneur in capitalistic state does not aim to satisfy in the best way the needs of the population, or to think of the interests of animals, plants and environment. Even if he is socially responsible and ecologically oriented businessman, he is not capable to respond in the best possible ways to the needs of the environment, because it would increase his costs incredibly and this could jeopardize his survival as an economic subject in the competitive conditions.

What are the problems that the capitalistic production process is causing?

If we examine from different perspectives a concrete example of economic production of a good, we will see how the whole process is affecting living beings. The production of chickens in modern capitalistic state illustrates visibly the way the modern economy functions and the problems that it creates. In this example is presented briefly the economic, trade and labor process in the most developed country in capitalistic sense - the United States of America.

If we use holistic approach for the objectives of the present analysis, we can conclude that in modern day poultry had been initiated many social challenges and are violated the interests of the subjects of the holistic model:

Violated interests of humankind

Below are pointed out some of the most significant violation of the interests of humankind.

1. The health of the workers in poultry factories is seriously affected. As a result performing their routine activities the health of the workers is irreparably harmed.[25] Respiratory diseases, infection, caused by the animals, as well as musculoskeletal injuries are just some of the negative effects on which are subjected the workers in the poultry factories.[26]

Despite that this information is well known to the corresponding corporations and responsible state institutions, real actions towards better protection of the human rights of the workers have not be taken. Health of humans and quality of life of the workers are issues, which are largely ignored in the whole economic branch of poultry and poultry products.

2. The labor which is performed does not develop enough the potentials of the workers and efforts on behalf of the employers in this direction are missing. One of the main duties of the worker in a poultry factory is to hook up 35 living chickens to metal shackles in one minute. This type of activity is performed between 8-12 hours a day. It is visible that this profession is not only very hard to work physically, but also contributes very little for the personal and social development of the individual.

---

25 Bureau of Labor Statistics (BLS), United States Department of Labor. Occupational Injuries and Illnesses and Fatal Injuries Profiles database queried by industry for Agriculture, Forestry, Fishing and Hunting (GP2AFH), Accessed June 2013

26 www.osha.gov/dsg/topics/agriculturaloperations/hazards_controls.html

3. The continuation of the working time and the low salaries of the workers in the poultry factories lead to diminished opportunities for access to goods and services as well as to limited possibilities for other entertaining or self-developing activities. Because the labor in not qualified the workers are remunerated with minimum or close to minimum wages in all states.

4. The continuation of the working time significantly limits the possibilities for positive social contact with their families and closed ones. If the worker is a parent and this hard labor takes 12 hours per day (including with the transportation) for him it would be much harder to communicate and bond with his children and his family partner. This could more often leads to problems in the family and in the process of raising the children. Considering the low wages of the workers, their families are put under stress of economic deprivation.

The governors of the capitalistic system are aware of all these effects of the economic process and their disrespect towards human life is blatant. The managers of the poultry factories are also aware that the low wages and harmful environment are damaging the life of the workers which means are violation of the interests of humankind. If people are willing to live in harmony, they should renounce this inhumane system and apply its alternative - the holistic model.

5. The interest of humankind is violated also in relation to the provision of healthy food for all people. On a worldwide scale livestock breeding has become an economic branch which is endangering the health of the people more and more. It is already proofed that the ways that some of the species are raised leads to meat which is not healthy for consumption.[27] Their organisms are becoming more resistant to the antibiotics, with which they are injected and according to a detailed research on Antibiotic Resistance and Food Animal Production this is endangering the health of people.[28] When the pro-

---

27 Silbergeld, E. K.; Graham, J.; Price, L. B. (2008). *Industrial Food Animal Production, Antimicrobial Resistance, and Human Health.* Annual Review of Public Health 29: 151–169

28 *Antibiotic Resistance and Food Animal Production: a Bibliography of Scientific Studies (1969-2012)* (PDF)

ducers of meat are aiming to maximize their profits, the health of animals and even people is always placed in the background. These are violations of the interest of humankind and of the concerned animal species.

6. According to Food and Agriculture Organization of the United Nations the registered production of chicken meat worldwide is around 108 million tones for 2014.[29]

The loss of production, which means edible meat that does not find its final consumer, is about 1/3 of all worldwide meat industry. In the regions with population with high income losses of meat reach 2/3 from the production.[30]

The total loss of food, including fruits and vegetables is at least 1.3 billion tons per year. This large quantity of edible food is more than enough to feed all malnourished people on the planet.

7. The direction of scientific research and development is oriented towards the selfish interests of large corporations, which are disregarding those of humankind and animals. Therefore, instead of improving the quality of life of humans and animals, involved in the mead industry, it is deteriorating. Scientists are funded to research and conduct unnatural genetic modifications of animals, creating stronger antibiotics and not to work on solving challenges of the relationship between humans and animals.

Violated interests of the animals

1. The life of the chickens, which are raised in poultry factories, is on average of six weeks. They are placed in dark spaces, often without windows, and this is causing fear and makes their short life into a prolonged agony.

2. The chickens are subjected to genetic modifications and on them are used drugs for faster and bigger growth. The obesity is so large that until the sixth week 90 % of them are unable to walk.

---

29 www.fao.org/ag/againfo/themes/en/meat/background.html
30 www.fao.org/docrep/018/i3347e/i3347e.pdf

3. In some of the larger factories the chickens are subjected to mutilations in the first ten day of their life. Their beaks are cut in order to avoid hurting other animals in this stressful environment. In many cases, while the chicken is alive are cut its limbs and combs. All these manipulations are performed without the usage of anesthetics, because it is cheaper.

This terrible attitude towards billions of living beings is a result of ruthless competition between corporations, which strive for survival and prosperity, because they are functioning in capitalistic system. The disregard of the interests of the animals is done in the name of the service to the self and in pursue of larger profit at all costs.

Violated interests of Earth

1. The production of food worldwide is the third largest polluter of the environment of Earth and it stands behind the whole economic production of United States and China. From the food wastage footprint report of FAO Globally, the blue water footprint (i.e. the consumption of surface and groundwater resources) of food wastage is about 250 km^3.[31]

2. At world level, the total amount of food wastage in 2007 occupied almost 1.4 billion hectares, equal to about 28 percent of the world's agricultural land area.[32]

These statistical numbers illustrate that the cycle of egoistic capitalistic economy is very ineffective and violates the interests of all four subjects of the holistic model.

Many more examples can be given by professionals in the corresponding areas - humanists, ecologists, animal rights defenders, resource management experts, climatologists, economists, etc.

It is well known that in order corporations to sell a product, they need to influence the demand by advertisement campaigns and complicated marketing strategies. At the same time, every salesman is avoiding to inform his customers the inconvenient information about the product and the process by which it is created. Low levels of consump-

---

31 www.fao.org/docrep/018/i3347e/i3347e.pdf
32 Ibid.

tion are not good for the economy and for the state. Everything in this picture is wrong!

We have to outline that corporations themselves are a controlled product which is raised in the competitive waters of capitalism. Therefore, states are the subjects, which are responsible for the creation of all these complex problems. The state is maintaining the economic environment and it stimulates the selfish attitudes of everyone in it. Corporation is the subject which implements the model and its actions are regulated by the law, the ethics of its management and by the market.

We have to point out clearly that despite the capitalistic environment of competition and constant risk from bankruptcy, it is precisely the private initiative of many people and of private corporations which have created and provided many of the goods which are developing humankind. Most of the goods and services that we use today are achieved because of private initiative and efforts of the employees of a corporation. The holistic approach does not aim to dismantle corporations and free private initiatives, but to support them by ennoblement of the environment. Improving of the economic climate, social and ecological guidance of private subjects, provision of state guarantees, if they are directed towards policies of service to the whole, are measures in this direction.

How would look like the process of poultry production, organized in the service to the whole?

In order to achieve optimal satisfaction of the interests of the subjects of the holistic model, the management activities, related to production and distribution of chickens should be conducted by applying the holistic approach on every stage. This means that the effect from every activity should correspond in the best way to the interest of humankind, animals, plants and Earth. Below are presented the principles and guidelines of the organization of this production process, so that it satisfies the interests of the whole. Many additional measures and guidelines can be adopted, which would improve the overall economic process. It is important to describe briefly the course of establishing the relationships between the participants and how to create such bonds which are satisfying their interests in the best possible way.

Satisfied interest of humankind

In order to be satisfied the real need of humankind from consumption of chicken meat, firstly should be collected detailed information how many participants of the holistic organization would like to consume the corresponding species for a certain period of time. In this way the resources, which are allocated for advertisement of poultry products, aiming to artificially increase their demand can be used for other purposes, which are more important for the holistic economy. Simple notification and informing of the population that poultry products with specific characteristics are available is required to evaluate the real needs of the final consumers.

After collecting this information the holistic organization is ready to initiate the management process for production and delivery of different poultry products for those participants, who desire to consume them. Applying this approach will simultaneously eliminate overproduction and shortage of food. At the same time animals would not be killed without purpose, or the environment would be polluted for the production of food, which nobody consumes in the end. Human labor for the production of products which do not have their consumer would also be saved.

The management of the holistic organization is supposed to plan additional food for reserves and for other purposes.

Organization of the labor process of the employee

To achieve real protection of human rights of the employee in the best possible way, it is necessary to determine such length of the working process, which is comfortable for him and provide enough time for other activities, social contacts, entertainments, etc. The guiding principle for norming of the working day is to provide the opportunities for the employee optimally to exercise his non-working activities. Therefore in the holistic organization should be legally regulated the shortest possible time in which the planned activities can be performed. In the example of the poultry factory this means to determine the number of working hours per person, based on the job descriptions and involved employees and to produce the planned poultry goods.

Dividing the working process of compulsory and voluntary time is significant for acknowledging the free will of all involved employees. On the stage of negotiating the contract with the employee he has to agree to work the compulsory time and he would be free to choose to work voluntarily in addition or not.

A detailed research is needed to determine the amount of compulsory time that the system can require from the employees. It should not be more than six hours per day. Every holistic organization will fix the compulsory time and it may be less than six hours, but should not be more than that. The employees would receive all public rights, including economic access to public goods which the organization is providing. This access is equal for all participants, without regards of their type of job position, hierarchical level and working experience, because the holistic model considers access to all public goods to be legal right for the people and not a form of reward. Labor relations are reviewed separately in chapter six.

Working in poultry factory would probably be unpleasant for most of the people and an unattractive job for them. Stimulus should not be by provision of larger access to goods, because this would be a violation of equality to such access with others. The solution for the holistic organization is to reduce the compulsory time for this job position and making it as much attractive and pleasant as possible for the employees.

If we accept that a working day of six hours is a reasonable balance between labor in service to the community and personal time, working in poultry factory should be less than that. The management of the holistic organization should estimate the needed amount of employees for this economic activity. For example Instead of two shifts of six hours per day, there can be three shifts of four hours per day. For comparison, presently 375,000 people are working in the field of poultry production only in the United States. They are producing around 9 billion chickens per year.[33]

Health of the workers is of primal importance for protecting the interest of humankind and it is an absolute necessity their work to be organized in such a way to avoid the high risks for health, which exists presently in capitalistic production.

---

33 https://www.uspoultry.org/economic_data/

Secondly, to satisfy the interest of humankind the poultry should be healthy products for all consumers and they should not carry high risks of infections, because of genetic modifications and harmful drugs which are present in the meat.

The next step of improving the satisfaction of the interest of humankind is related with reducing the loss of food and distributing it to those in need.

In a well-developed holistic economy all participants would receive equal access to goods against their main responsibility to provide specific labor, which is beneficial for the whole.

Satisfied interest of the animals

In order to achieve optimal protection of the interest of the animals, it is important to approach them with respect, kindness and humane treatment. This attitude is especially needed for those species, which are going to be used as a resource for humans. Responsibility of humankind is to protect the corresponding animal species in sufficient quantity as well as in its best quality - by preserving its natural genetic heritage.

The interaction with animals in a holistic organization should be with respect as with living creatures, which are emotional and not as if they are senseless objects what we see in the present.

First of all animals are part of the whole and secondly - some of them are necessary resource for the survival of humankind. After we tune ourselves to this vision it is logical to improve the way of life animals are having, including those which are set for consumption. Holistic production requires the creation of environment which is optimally pleasant for them; providing normal length of life, feeding them with healthy food and using the most painless ways of ending their lives. It is in the interest of animals their genetic heritage not to be modified.

Satisfied interest of the plants

In the process of raising chickens it is necessary to be regarded the interest of affected plant species. If some of the activities are jeopardizing the life of a particular plant, they should be changed in such a way so that is avoided. An example of such activities is building a poultry factory on a territory, which is very suitable for life of particular plants. In the process of reducing CO_2 emissions and the water imprint from the production, it would have direct positive effect on the preservation of plants.

Satisfied interest of the Earth's environment

The interest of Earth is the next, which should be taken into consideration in the system of service to the whole in the management of every process, including poultry production. Experts in the corresponding fields should prepare clear criteria for maximum allowed levels of pollution, when it is inevitable for the particular time period and technological development. In the concrete example it would be needed to choose the most suitable land on which should be built the factory. Many factors should be taken into account, so that the interests of the other subjects of the holistic model are also respected. It is necessary to be made analysis whether a particular are is not more needed for other purposes with higher priority, whether it is large enough for providing living space for the animals, whether the workers would have easy access to the factory, etc.

By organizing the manufacturing process in a way which significantly reduces the CO_2 imprint, the interest of Earth would be much better protected than it is today. This means that new type of ecological production should be implemented with new technologies. This need would have to direct the scientific studies and research focus instead of corporate greed.

Protection of Earth's environment means also to reduce the water imprint in all of the production processes.

Applying holistic approach in the economy and respecting the interests of humankind, animals, plants and Earth, would lead to gradual integration of all economic branches and to reducing the pollution of Earth. For example if the management of the holistic organization is directing the scientific development towards discovering ecological ways of transportation, this would be beneficial for the environment of the particular area, but also for the ecological condition of the world.

Presently, there is not a legal or technological impediment to be massively introduced renewable energetic resources in all economic sectors. This act would have lower the manufacturing costs of all products and would be beneficial for the environment. The preservation of the modern capitalistic system in which one of the richest corporations are the oil companies, cannot lead to such positive actions.

The advantages of the holistic production over capitalistic one are obvious and some of the most important can be listed as follows:

1. The energetic balance of Earth remains intact, biological species are not destroyed, soils, water and air are not polluted, or at least polluted in minimum.

2. Plants and animals which are set to be used as part of the food industry of humankind and animals would be far less than they are today. Those which would be placed in farms and factories shall receive respectful treatment and the opportunity for good life. Their species would not be threatened from extinction or harmful genetic manipulation. Holistic economy has the purpose to maintain equilibrium and to preserve all species.

3. The production of all goods and services is made with the aim to answer concrete needs, expressed by the individuals and to be beneficial and healthy for the people. This means that compromise with the quality that we see today for most products would not be necessary. It would not be needed to use dangerous chemicals and genetic modifications in order to create meat with more pleasant look. It would not be necessary to create dependence of the consumers upon certain products to guarantee corporate survival. It would not be necessary to create food with grater durability on the expense of good taste, because every product would be on demand.

4. Efforts would be made to organize the production and distribution of food which is desired and healthy by the participants.

5. Through introduction of holistic economy would be limited overproduction, which means better management of resources. This includes better management of human labor on issues which are with priority for the organization. Good governance would lead to less workload for the employee. In the absence of overproduction and ecological provision of needed goods Earth would be used efficiently. The result would be calm existence of other biological species on Earth.

6. Classifying the needs and not the people will provide an opportunity to use public resources to create those goods and services

which are most pertinent at the time. This is true equality in which public goods are accessible for everyone in the same way. The global implementation of this principle will result in avoiding starvation and malnutrition of billions of people.

7. Another important advantage of the holistic economy over capitalistic one is the inclusion of sufficient amount of people in the economy, using the most advanced technologies and acknowledging the limitations of compulsory working time which cannot be more than six hours per day.

8. In a holistic economy there is no unemployment and people are not exploited for the selfish desires of someone to have more things.

9. Scientific development is not jeopardizing job positions and the survival of people. It would be directed to achieve better satisfaction of the interests of the whole and not to increase the gap between rich minority and poor majority.

4. Legal regime of ownership

,, How can you buy or sell the sky, the warmth of the land? The idea is strange to us. If we do not own the freshness of the air and the sparkle of the water, how can you buy them? Every part of this earth is sacred to my people. Every shining pine needle, every sandy shore, every mist in the dark woods, every clearing and humming insect is holy in the memory and experience of my people... This we know, the Earth does not belong to man, man belongs to the Earth, this we know. All things are connected"

Part of the speech of Chief Seattle in 12.01.1854 as written in notes of Henry Smith

If there is a question which is of key importance to make distinctions in the philosophies of both types of systems, this is the correlation of public and private property and specifically: the purpose of public property for the needs of the whole.

Let's focus our attention on the philosophy behind the legal regime of public and private property in modern capitalistic societies for satisfaction of the needs of the people. The same principle is implemented in all states and it can be summarized as the following: Needs of the people are satisfied through the exchange of private property. This means that people are buying their homes, automobiles, food, clothes, medicaments, entertainments and other goods from private corporations. Most of the resources for their lives are dependent on being capable to pay the asked price.

The fundamental problem in using private property to satisfy basic needs of the people is that the driving force of the supplier of the good is his personal interest, which means that he serves his ego. The interest of the receiver of the good is secondary and those of Earth, future generations and the other subjects of the holistic model are completely disregarded. If capitalistic state recognizes some of these interests, it tries to regulate them on purpose, but it is impossible to achieve the best result, because for the private corporations these are additional costs and not a form of service to the whole.

The corporation which produces food could not be competitive enough, if it protects in the best way the interest of the environment, the animals and plants as well as the interest of the future generation of people. This corporation does not have to be interested whether all people are fed and whether the quality of food is high, because these are global political and humanitarian issues. The corporation which produces food has only one objective - to continue its present on the market, to grow by taking advantage on the fact that people need food.

Therefore, the capitalistic state indirectly delegates to the private property the purpose to satisfy public needs. Despite this expectation of the state, there is no legal obligation of the private subject to satisfy those needs and this is not its motivation for existence.

The argument that the state defines the rules of governing of the private property and by setting requirements and limitations it satisfies indirectly the public needs is correct in a very small part. If the capitalistic state was capable to solve by regulations all social and environmental problems, which are emerging from economic production, why do they exist? The reasons are well-known and the main is that corporations do not want to increase their expenses and are using all political and economic leverages to avoid additional regulations, which are related with long-term benefits for society which are not going to bring profit.

The private property in all countries has at least three common characteristics on which is not placed much attention:

• Every private property was public at some point in the past and if certain legal conditions are met it can also be expropriated by the state again. Such transformation of property back to public is usually followed equal indemnification of the private subject. This characteristic of the private property can be defined as "relative independence" of the owner to manage it. The obligation to protect the private property is declared as a supreme value in capitalistic societies, but in fact there are no juridical boundaries the property to be taken by the owner on the abstractly defined grounds for public needs.

• The second characteristic is that private property is always bringing financial burden for the owner which is an income for the state. These are the taxes and obligations for good governance. The amount is defined solely by the state which can always make private property to become an excessive burden for the owner, if the state desires that. In ordinary circumstances this form of pressure is weak, because one of its purposes is to serve as stimulus for good governance of the property and the inclusion of the owner in the market economy, besides being an income for the state. This characteristic can be defined as "financial burden" of the private property. It stimulates the owner to make it a quoted commodity, without regards whether it is useful for humankind and the environment. In this way the owner becomes highly dependent from the market forces, which are determining the value of his property.

• The third main characteristic of the private property in the capitalistic system is that its value is always mutable upon the influence of the market. The interconnection of the global economy and financial systems turns all types of property to become vulnerable to lose their value, depending on the moods of the market. This characteristic can be defined as "uncertainty of the value". The price of every property is formed by market relationships. This means that if an employee would like to acquire goods and services which are needed for him and his family, he is completely dependent from the fact that the market is evaluating his labor or service he is providing for society. It is irrelevant how important and useful is this service in reality. This inhumane distortion of the ethics of capitalism always places on the top of the egoistic pyramid those who are greedy, unscrupulous, speculative and exploitive of others. Most of the people, who are striving for life, based on natural human relationships and provision of services, which are beneficial for society, are placed on lower levels of economic prosperity and institutional capacity to influence. The reason is that they would not make compromises with lives and suffering of other people in the name of larger profit. In many cases the rising in the social ladder of capitalistic system is accompanied with ethical degradation and spiritual self-destruction, because people are invited to act inhumanely.

In capitalistic societies public property is used for administrative needs of the state, for large infrastructure, energetic and national security projects. Despite that by definition this property is public in many cases it is governed in the same way as the private - citizens have to pay for its usage. Let's take for example the management of nuclear power plant, which is owned by the state. This means that the state has used public resources for its building, for the land, for hiring the employees and for all other activities to make this project work. Even though that the state took the money of its own citizens, the produced amount of electricity is sold to the same citizens on market prices. For the population there is no difference whatsoever whether the property is public or private, because they would have to pay the same price in both cases.

In capitalistic societies is proclaimed the statement that state is a poor manager of its property and therefore it is necessary to privatize it or granting it of concessions. The state truly in many cases is a poor manager because of corruption of its representatives, incompetency and indifference of state officials, but this is a problem of the rules for appointment of unprepared people for certain positions, weakness of judicial organs to establish crimes and administrative violations. There are no stricter guarantees that state officials would not be corrupted in relation to gathering taxes, but this activity always remains public. When public property is privatized it can easily go in the hands of every other state or private actor that is willing to exploit it for selfish reasons.

Public interest is not protected in capitalistic societies firstly, because it is vague, not clearly defined and is replaced with an understanding of a collection of dominating private interests.

The holistic model, on which would be created holistic organizations, foresees clear regulation and distinction between public and private property in their purpose and managing principles.

The state is a poor manager in the capitalistic system, because high official positions are taken by people, who are convenient for parties and big corporations. In holistic organization career development is dependent entirely on the expert qualities and the ethics of the person.

In holistic organizations public property is meant to develop the whole, by satisfying the interests of the subjects of the holistic model. Therefore, most of the public property and the products created by it are equally accessible to all participants in order to satisfy their needs. Public property in a holistic organization is not privatized and it is not granted for concession, because selfish management of private actors would violate the interests of the whole. The privatizer or the concessioner would use the property to gain profit from it. Instead of giving away its public property, the holistic organization shall seek to employ the best managers, to apply the most useful innovations, to adapt the highest ecological standards and to use the property with respect to the most pertinent needs of the whole.

The definition of public interest in capitalistic state is much narrower than the interest of the whole. The first includes only the benevolence of the nation and it can be described also as egoistic one, because it competes with interest of other nations.

What would happen, if the state begins to manage its public property in a way which satisfies by priority of classes the needs of all participants and in the interest of the whole?

The holistic state should apply the principles of holistic governance towards its participants, but in foreign relations it should not engage in activities which are violating the interests of humankind, animals, plants and Earth. Consequently, the holistic state has not right to use cocoa and chocolate products, which are produced with violation of children's rights. In general it should not buy or sell products, which were created with violation of human rights. Such commercial relations and economic connections contradict the interest of the whole and the holistic state has to find lasting solutions and build new alternatives for acquiring these goods.

In the example of the production of food, the following criteria should be taken into account:

- How many people have declared that they need the concrete food for certain period of time?

- Which is the most humane way of producing the food?

- Which is the most ecological process of its production?

- Which is the most humane process of farming animals and plants?

- Which are the most efficient and ecological ways of logistics of the food to the consumers?

- What percentage of this food should be used for reserve and for future members of the community?

The holistic approach of producing food on demand by implementing global planning and regarding the interests of all living beings will result in much better results than capitalistic system of competition between private actors is capable of.

If the capitalistic economy can be compared with a competition and fight for survival, the holistic economy resembles a symphony orchestra, which creates and performs music that elevates the human spirit and brings people harmony and joy.

4.1. Private property in the holistic organization

The purpose of the private property is to serve the owner for his personal use. Next to it should not be attached the expectations to satisfy public needs. The holistic organization appreciates and respects private property and the right of everyone to possess and to freely use his property in compliance with the legal regime. Even more, the holistic state eliminates the possibilities for its expropriation which do exist in capitalistic economy. The reason is that the state possesses much more property than any private citizen and it has to manage it for the benefit of all participants and in the interest of the whole. The holistic state should always respect and guarantee the right of people to use their private property freely. It should not be allowed sanctions against unlawful behavior to include confiscation of private property. This is significant advantage of the holistic model over the capitalistic, because respect of human rights and economic freedoms exists even for people who have committed criminal act or administrative wrongdoings. In capitalistic states financial sanctions and confiscation are considered as normal form of punishment for unlawful behavior. Private property can become public again in a holistic state only after donation which is made freely by the owner.

The second advantage in managing private property in a holistic state is that it is not necessary to be subjected to high taxing burden, which is typical for capitalism. The holistic state possesses its own property and it can produce enough goods and services from it. Good governance of public resources in holistic organization would lead to the situation that it depends much less from trade between private actors and taxes. The ability to produce and distribute variety of goods and services would make the holistic state strong and independent. It would not be necessary to rely on redistributing the wealth of others as is its role in capitalism.

This approach would lower the financial burden over private owners significantly and their future uncertainty that the tax policies of the state could be changed in their disadvantage. Therefore, it would be fair to conclude that the holistic organization provides better regime for owners of private property than we see in capitalistic countries today.

Despite these advantages, which come from easing the tax burden over private property and the uncertainty for its excessive taxation, in the holistic economy would need much less the commercial activities of private actors. The reason is that gradually all public needs would have to be satisfied by the holistic state and it should be done for free - without selling or crediting. This means that a person or an organization which would like to become rich by managing their private property, taking advantage on the needs of others, would find strong competitor in the face of a holistic organization. This difficulty of the private sector comes from the fact that the holistic organization aims to satisfy the needs of its participants for free, as a human right they do deserve. If a person is a member of a holistic organization, he has the right to receive equal access to public products together with other members. In this case we can safely assume that he is not going to buy similar products from private companies.

The possibility the private property to be traded should always be protected by the holistic state and parallel existence of both types of properties should be legally guaranteed. Private initiative and entrepreneurship would be able to develop, but private interest should not be capable to distort the interest of the whole. Preservation of both regimes of ownership and the opportunity for internal trade are important conditions for safeguarding the freedom of people to create new goods with their own resources, to trade them and to make profit from their work.

Parallel existence of both types of approaches in a holistic organization is going to be an important indicator to what extent its members are oriented in the service to the ego and to what in service to the whole. This would be an indispensible tool for evaluating the trust in the organization and its leadership and to observe the level of personal development of people. The result would be that private entrepreneur will be free to use his own resources for the creation of a product which he can sell to make a profit. However, if a private entrepreneur would like to create a product which can be available for all who are willing to use it for free, the holistic organization would provide all needed resources and include it in the list of products for distribution. In this way the creative spark would not be distorted, according to the market or to the will of investors and creditors.

Participants of every holistic organization are always free to leave. If the organization is poorly managed, people can try to go back to capitalistic relationships and sell their labor.

The inability of a person or an organization to acquire certain good immediately is the fundament on which is built the banking system in capitalism. This leads to multiple rising of the expenses of all economic process - from production, to buying and reselling, credits for all subjects on the chain. For example if a person desires to buy a house with credit, he is going to pay two or three times the price that the seller requires, which means he has to work two to three times more to satisfy his basic need of accommodation. The construction company sells the building for two to three times more than he has used to build it in order to make a profit and to return credits which he might have taken. This means that the person who is buying the house pays four to six times its cost. If this person is an employee of a private corporation and he relies on his salary, this means that this corporation has to earn four to six times more money in order to satisfy the greed of a construction company and a bank, so that its employee has an accommodation.

The banking system of credit with interest is a burden for the whole capitalistic system and for all people, because they are placed in a financial framework of permanent indebtedness.

All legal subjects, with the exception of central banks, owe money, which means that their behavior is dependent from their creditors. This debt is a fundamental weakness which can be exploited by banking institutions.

The inability of a person to receive certain goods when he needs them is the reason why he is looking for funding. At this moment baking institutions break the natural creative initiative of the person to make something good for society and for the whole which may never bring back profit. They replace it with the attitude to search a way to return your debt. Which bank is going to credit a painter to create a masterpiece, which can be dedicated to inspire future generations?

In a holistic organization the decisions which project to be secured with real resources (not with finances) should be taken in the context of the driving force of service to the whole and not necessarily bringing economic return and profit. Projects are selected when they contribute to development of the organization and harmonizing the environment and the initiator of the project proposes and arguments the direction. The creator or the person who is willing to serve with his labor is seen as a contributor for positive change in society and not as a debtor to the holistic organization, which is providing the resources.

Presently, people are enforced or at least encouraged not to think how to contribute positively for society, but to focus on their own survival and to find ways of returning their debt. People are not thought to protect the interest of humankind, which is placed in service to the whole. They are put in permanent debt from which they have to search of salvation.

The main functions of banking institutions are to increase the debt of the population and to credit projects in service to the ego. In this way they are making people, corporations and nations to desire to be sold and used.

The vulnerability of the person in debt and of the seeker of resources detaches him from higher ideals and from the global perspective of interest of humankind. In capitalistic economic environment people are losing their sensitivity for the suffering of others and they become incapable to react constructively to all forms of violation of interests of humankind, animals, plants and Earth. People become weak to react even against violation of their personal human rights. In order to be discontinued this policy of division and compartmentalization of society it is necessary the goods created by public resources to be made and distributed with complete regard to the interest of the subjects of the holistic model. The survival of capitalism relies on artificial maintenance of limited access to goods. The next prerequisite is that the participants have to desire to consume more and to possess more luxury goods, which can be randomly changed. Economic growth and constantly rising consumption are an absolute necessity for the capitalistic system, but they are not necessarily useful for the development of society. The above enumerated features of the egoistic system, which we can conclude as problems for humanity and the planet, are its imminent and indispensible preconditions for lasting existence. They could never be eliminated from this system, because they are defining it.

How would be functioning capitalism, if there is a "free lunch" - if public resources are used for the creation of goods which are distributed to all participants as their human right?

People, raised with the values of capitalism, would think of such scenario as a disaster, because fear for survival and competition in an unpredictable environment are denuded. Many people still think that coercion and pressure are the most appropriate forms of stimulation of society and they are turning the economic wheel. For their level of perceiving the world it would be impossible to imagine society in which people are freed from these forces.

For the holistic economy growth is not an end itself and consumption at all cost is not stimulated. It is harmful to misbalance the natural needs of people and to satisfy them in an unequal order. In front of the holistic economy is placed the aim of satisfaction of the needs of all participants, so that they can develop and feel happy. Organization of labor and of economy on a holistic model will demonstrate not only that it is possible for significant part of society, but also that this will lead to much larger economic growth, stability of the environment, humane treatment of the employees, spiritual development of people, reduction of crime, elimination of poverty and unemployment, protection of all other biological species and the long-term solution of the global challenges of today, such as climate change.

4.2. Public property in the holistic state

The state which functions as a holistic organization has to manage its public property in the service to the whole. There is a significant difference between management in the service to the whole and in narrowly formulated national interest. The last is typical for capitalism. Modern definition of the public property of the state does not provide any guarantees for its management for the benefit of all citizens. Even less guarantees exist that public resources will not be used against the interest of humankind and other subjects of the holistic model.

The state which adopts the holistic model is responsible for providing directly goods and services and management of public property is crucial for this function. The question arises: is it necessary to transform the public property into private in the process of provision of these goods and services?

If the answer is positive, this would mean that the participants would be free to transfer this property to other people, who might not be sharing the values and ideals of the holistic community. This could jeopardize the interest of the holistic organization and unduly deprive its participants from the right to use these goods.

The second risk in eventual transformation of the property from public to private would emerge, if the participant decides at some point to leave the organization. He is free to choose so and he is free to take all his possessions. Such voluntary relinquishment would result in decrease of the property of the holistic organization, if the received goods are transformed to private property.

Thirdly, every participant receives certain goods from the holistic organization as a form of exercising a right, so that his needs and desires are met. If this person would like to support other people and desires to sell or donate his goods, he may apply to work for the corresponding department of the holistic organization and not redistributes his goods.

If a person desires to acquire other products from the capitalistic market by using the goods that he has received by right, he would probably need to work for the foreign trade department of the holistic organization and to trade in the interest of the holistic organization and in the interest of the whole. In case that the person desires to profit only for himself from the received goods from the organization, his participation is under question, because the motivation for inclusion in the community is mismatching with the aim of the organization.

For these reasons it is logical to assume that the holistic community has to maintain the right over the property of all goods and services, which are created with public resources, but it has to provide exclusive rights to all users. These rights include inviolability, which is a feature of the private property. The person would not be able to sell or donate in order to avoid decreasing of the property of the holistic organization. Naturally, such actions are permitted with their private property.

Rights of the people are guaranteed much more than they are in capitalistic state. For example, in a holistic organization every participant has the right to receive abode with equally high quality with all others at all times. This means that in a holistic system the state would not confiscate it and would not leave the person homeless in tough times. In extraordinary cases, if change is required for a participant, it has to be negotiated with him and after his approval he has to be proposed another home, which serves best his needs. Capitalistic legal systems foresee the possibility for involuntary expropriation of private property and its substitution with similar one, whereas holistic organizations always respect the free will of the person and need his agreement for the proposed change. Therefore, the participant in a holistic organization is much more than a tenant or privileged user. He has the right to choose all goods and services available for him and to order them on demand. The goods and services which he receives are not directly related to his work and in case of illness or impossibility to perform labor, the participant would not be left on the streets and with lower access to goods, as will happen in capitalistic societies.

One of the positive effects of preserving the produced goods and services as public property is that they cannot be financially burdened, if the holistic organization is a sovereign state. There cannot be mortgages or guaranties of these goods. Their purpose is to satisfy the need of the particular person. This means that the person will never lose them and cannot gamble them.

4.3. Inheritance in a holistic organization

Generally adopted legal principles of inheritance of private property should remain the same in the holistic state.

When the issue is related with public property of a holistic organization, which was distributed for the needs of a particular person, it is important to be recognized the emotional connection and attachment to this object. After his death the will of the person should be taken into consideration how to be used the property by the organization. If the case refers to the granted home for the person and his family, his will would have to be regarded by the holistic organization in relation who has the right to continue living there. Such will is similar to the testamentary in the inheritance law, but the difference is that the property remains to the holistic organization. If such will is not made, the organization has to choose how to use the home, considering the emotional attachment of the diseased and the needs of his family.

5. Holistic organization and commercial relationships

From the viewpoint of the private person commercial relationships in the capitalistic state are means from financial income, personal survival and enrichment. From the perspective of the state however commerce has different significance and the main is provision of a variety of goods and services for the needs of the population. Commerce is an expression of the free economic initiative and it contributed hugely to the development of the civilization. Despite the achievements which are result from national and international trade, the egoistic mentality ignores the fact that before a piece of land to become private property of a person, or a capital asset for a company, it is part of Earth. Before plants and animals to be categorized as objects which are cultivated, cut and packed, they are living beings with own spiritual path of evolution. The adoption of the worldview of honoring nature and its biological species will lead to the emergence of the first holistic communities in which commercial activities will be fundamentally transformed.

In capitalistic societies goods are valued, if they can lead to growth of the capital, which is the financial appraisement. Therefore it signifies how desired is a particular object by financially solvent persons. Capital is a number which points out how much energy a company can take from others, taking advantage from the products it possesses. Therefore growth of the capital does not necessarily mean more goods, but it can signify more value of the same goods, resulted from higher demand.

The holistic system does not focus on financial value of its goods, but on their characteristics, equality of distribution among its participants and satisfaction of the interest of the whole in the process of their production, consumption and processing. It is justified that some of the goods of the holistic organization can be used for commercial activities with foreign subjects.

Commercial activities with persons outside of the holistic organization should always be an ideological and political instrument for achieving its aim - betters satisfaction of the interests of the whole. As was mentioned above, part of the property of the holistic organization would not be distributed among the participants, because their needs are met and this property is supposed to be used for foreign trade. These goods and services should be sold, exchanged or donated to particular persons, with pursuing clearly defined objectives. Commerce, which is conducted exclusively for profit, should not be an intrinsic line of thought for representatives of the holistic organization, because it would become another commercial entity, which is seeking to take energy from others to secure its survival.

The whole public resource of the holistic organization is managed in a way to satisfy the need of all participants, internal trade would not have this primal function of provision of variety of goods and services that exists in capitalistic societies. If the predominant property for production of goods and services is public and it is managed to guarantee equal access for the participants, internal trade between private actors would probably decrease significantly, because the demand would be met by free supply. This does not mean that internal trade should be banned or artificially restricted in the holistic organization. It is one of the freedoms that should be protected, but it would not be the backbone of economy and the main means for provision of goods for the participants.

The holistic organization aims to create an environment in which all its members are feeling themselves fully satisfied from their work and not be exploited by corporations, which are looking for profit at all costs.

Since the holistic organization retains ownership over the produced goods and services, the people who are receiving them for personal use are not their owners and therefore they cannot trade them. In this way people would not be motivated to block the access to goods for someone and to take selfish advantage from this situation in order to profit or make the person dependent. The principles for distribution have to be defined in advance to avoid misuse of official position which is so typical for capitalistic and communistic societies.

In foreign relations commercial relations and their avoidance have to be performed by holistic organizations always on ideological, ethical and political grounds. Unlike capitalistic societies in which financial system and international trade are *de facto* main priority of the states, but formally are separated from politics and international relations, in the holistic society foreign trade is conducted to implement policies and political objectives. It is impossible to achieve the political objectives of better satisfaction of the interests of the subjects of the holistic model without global management of all economic and trade process of the property of the holistic organization. This management includes coordination and planning on the highest political level. The meaning of the word "politics" in the context of the holistic system doesn't correspond with the negative "Machiavellian" connotation which exist in the egoistic societies - arbitrary autocracy, grabbing power for own sake, competition between parties, manipulation and misuse of official position, etc. In a holistic organization political are all actions of the participants, which are conducted on purpose to satisfy the interests of the subjects of the holistic model. They can be very diverse - from ordinary cooking of a meal through selection of the food and usage of energy for its preparation to the choice of transportation to work, etc.

In the same way the conscious participation in trade has very powerful political influence, when it is performed by consumers or merchants. It is precisely the purposeful refusal of large groups of people to buy goods, produced by corporation with certain nationality has led to some of the most significant political changes worldwide. The success of such actions is clearly visible in Swadeshi movement in India, as well as South African boycott of products with the aim to abolition of apartheid. The linking of humane ideological demands with economic actions is one of the most effective instruments for the success of just political cause. The applying of conscious choice for commercial activities is useful on an individual level and not only as a form of state sanctions. When the cause is just and the population of a country is aware of it, the refusal to buy certain goods is a key political act for social development. People, who are part of a holistic organization, should investigate thoroughly the energy which stands behind every commercial product. This energy includes but is not limited to the relationships between people and treatment of all living beings during all stages of creation and placement of this product. On a higher level of self-awareness of the connection with the whole people will be able to understand the motivation for trade of a particular person, as well as other forms of "energetic burdens" which a product has. Such "energetic burdens" might be violations of human rights in the process of production; excessive pollution of the environment; usage of components, which are harmful for health; the product is created with the intention to make the consumer dependent on it, etc.

If in the overall economic process exists the intention of better satisfaction of the interests of the subjects of the holistic model, then the commercial activities with foreign persons would be guided by the idea of service and not of taking advantage. Trade is a form of voting. It can be a means for improvement of the whole environment and key instrument for influencing foreign subjects.

The participant of holistic organization should be a deeply conscious consumer, who is researching the merchants, their labor practices; methods of production; plans for investments, political donations and other ways with which they are influencing the world. If such detailed information is missing or misleading, the final stage is avoidance of buying their products. This means that commercial activities are bound with certain ethical criteria which the consumer is searching from the merchant. There is no legal or moral hindrance these measures to be applied in modern capitalistic societies. There is no international treaty, investment partnership agreement, or law that can make a self-aware person to buy something.

Main principle can be deducted and it is that **trade relations in holistic organization always pursue ethical and political objectives and are key instrument for impact of foreign subjects in the interest of the whole**.

The aim of building these commercial bonds overlaps the purpose of the holistic organization: better satisfaction of the interests of the subjects of the holistic model in the organization and outside of it.

The exercising of commercial relations on behalf of people and organizations for achieving political objectives can be classified of passive and active, depending on their type of participation in the process. Passive participation represents one or more people to boycott certain product and abstain from its usage in order not to support activities for its production which are harmful to the whole. In practicing such boycott actions must be peaceful, thoughtful and targeted and not aggressive, hostile and chaotic. To be successful certain boycott, it is needed to be chosen a corporation, which is causing negative impact and success is to achieve clearly set objectives of holistic production, trade, consumption and recycling of products.

The strength of the consumer is in his choice and the ability to exist without most of the proposed products. The weakness of corporations is in their dependence from constant buying of their products in larger quantities. Even slight decrease of sales leads to harsh challenges of the corporation, respectively to its shareholders, creditors and countries in which it operates.

When such self-awareness is present among critical mass of society and good organizational management in the form of holistic organizations, the consumers would be able to influence many policies in their society.

Active participation in commercial relations includes that the choice of the consumer to buy certain goods to be bound with demands of holistic production. In this case it is important that the consumer has access to information from thorough audit. It is not enough declaration of the corporation that legislation of certain country is obeyed. It is not enough the promises of managers that donations will be made to non-governmental organizations. This information can be obtained after thorough audit of the whole production process and verification whether particular financial resources are distributed as declared. Active participation includes also careful selection of commercial partners and strict agreements among them of applying holistic principles in the production of the products, protecting labor rights of people, their access to goods, ecological standards of production and all other components, mentioned above.

Logically such audits are suitable to be performed by professionally prepared auditors, who are observing not just the legislation, but also the holistic criteria, which are established to engage in commercial trade. Consequently, these are much deeper partnerships which are the basis for deeply integrated commercial relations than the *fair trade* agreements, for example. In the last are only implemented minimum threshold of prices of the products, which guarantee better conditions for producers. If certain corporation is not willing to share information on these parameters to trade partners and consumers, commercial relationships with it should be avoided. It has to be mentioned here that presently there are working mechanisms for achieving better satisfaction of the interests of the whole through independent audits of the corporations, but they are not effective enough in the global economy, because violation of rights in many cases leads to lower costs of production and makes the products more competitive. Competition and lower governmental control in many states lead to the fact that many of the products that we consume today are made with harsh violation of the interests of humankind, such as slavery, child labor, extreme working conditions, etc. Transformation of the whole process would be impossible without active role of the consumers and without observation of strict laws for protection of people and nature.

Commercial relations from the viewpoint of a holistic organization can be differentiated into three separate groups:

1. Internal trade - between members of the holistic organization;
2. External trade - between holistic organization and external subjects;
3. Trade between holistic organizations.

5.1. Principles of internal trade relations

The holistic organization exists with the clear aim to create harmonious environment for its participants in order to provide the conditions for their positive self-expression and happiness. As in the loving family it is not accepted its members to trade between each other, so in the holistic community it is not encouraged selfish trade interaction between its participants. The reason is that in most cases trade is aimed at profit and interest of the self. The next consideration of not encouragement of internal trade is related with the creation of products. As was pointed above, the holistic organization is responsible for the protection of the interests of humankind, animals, plants and Earth from resource extraction, to production, distribution, consumption and recycling. For a private corporation or a sole merchant these conditions and global interests are negligible, because they are increasing the costs, over-pricing the products and reducing the profit. The desire of a person to create goods which are beneficial for society and for the whole is the guiding motivation which is stimulated in the holistic society. This is the economic motor that will move the holistic organization and its participants. Commercial relations inside holistic organization should be allowed and to them it is prudent to be applied the principles of taxing in capitalism. However, taxes should not be the main source of income for holistic organization, as it has to manage its public property in the service to the whole.

5.2. Principles of external trade relations

Important, but not exclusive, is the function of the trade relations with an external subject to provide needed goods and services for the holistic organization and its participants. These are goods which the organization is unable to produce at this particular moment. Trade and not free access to public goods should be the norm with external persons, because they have expressed the desire to live according to the principles of capitalism and to remain foreign for the holistic society. At the same time all external subjects are perceived as part of the whole and potential members of the holistic society. For these reasons even though that the holistic organization is not responsible for these states, international organizations, private corporations and people, trade with them should be conducted in a way which are in the interest of the whole. Therefore, relationships have to be built with careful consideration of the interests of the members of the holistic community and those of the external subjects. The motivation of the representative of a holistic organization for trade should never be just for profit, but should include humanitarian and ecological aspects. This means that are needed much more evaluations to determine whether to trade with someone and what would be the overall effects of such actions. Precondition for trade with external partners is access to information about their economic and labor process and ecological practices. This information is needed in order to evaluate the effect of the corresponding organizations and to determine whether interests of the whole would be better satisfied in eventual commerce. This form of mutual monitoring is extraneous for capitalistic relationships, because corporations are protecting the trade secrets of their products. This privacy allows them to conceal violation of human rights. Capitalism requires trade secrets, because all subjects are in a state of rigorous competition and every innovation and good practice can lead to strategic advantage in economic or political sense. The holistic system is structured on completely different fundament and it is related to mandatory transparency. This free access to information is needed for all trade partners and consumers in order to justify in front of them that the economic process is holistic. Otherwise, trade partners could be corporations which are committing violating of human rights and the economic chain would become contaminated.

In the example of the cocoa production the holistic organization should avoid supply with cocoa from corporations and states in which there are evidences of violation of human rights and particularly children's rights, low wages and low level of ecological innovation. If a corporation or a state desire to trade with a holistic organization they have to reorganize their whole production processes on a holistic model. This requirement makes trade as an instrument for positive political transformation and development with respect to the living beings and the planet. Sovereign rights of all states are acknowledged and guaranteed by the international law and the holistic organizations should always respect this primal institute which protects the right of every country to choose its own path of development.

The holistic organization is responsible to evaluate what would be the consequences of supplying certain goods to capitalistic subjects and the effect of buying specific goods from them. If the overall effect is in the service to the whole such commercial activities should be allowed.

5.3. Trade relations between holistic organizations

Trade relations between holistic organizations are at the same time external, but also with a subject which has declared appurtenance to the satisfaction of the interest of the subjects of the holistic model. These relations are part of the holistic system and it is justified to have status *sui generis*. They are not entirely external and internal for a holistic organization.

Logically, the existence of such relations is possible only when there is more than one holistic organization. If the organizations have declared common goal of service to the whole, it is important to initiate cooperation between them. If there is unity in understanding of their common values, it is natural to move towards gradual integration of their economies and societies in general. This means that commercial activities would be first step in establishing strong relationships. The process of integration is voluntary and should be based on agreements. Important principle in its developing is to retain complete or almost complete independence from capitalistic subjects - corporations or states.

In the beginning holistic organizations would be created in capitalistic states which do have their own tax policy and it has to be observed. Legality, transparency and high ethical code should be intrinsic features of all holistic organizations.

In order to achieve its long-term goals and short-term objectives, the holistic society should develop itself, applying the principle of economic self-sufficiency, efficient and ecological management of the public resources. Trade relations with other holistic organizations should lead to growing of their economies, but should not be created risks from these actions. This means that trade relations should not be made in currencies of states, not to use securities which are bound with capitalistic subjects and all other instruments which are hiding risks from destabilization of the economies of the holistic organizations.

Petroleum products and oil as main energetic commodity in the capitalistic societies should be completely replaced as a good, when its alternatives are well developed, because it is the resource from which emerge the unhealthiest economic, political and even religious dependencies.

The implementation of the principle of economic self-sufficiency is of crucial importance for protection of the independence of the economy of the holistic organization, but also for the other subjects it is bond with.

It is fair to assume that trade relations between holistic organizations would be based on much bigger level of trust and closer cooperation, than relations with capitalistic subjects.

6. Principles of taxing policy in the holistic organizations

Taxing policy is a prerogative of the states and only they can determine which activities will be taxed and how much. It is the modus of the capitalistic state to procure economic goods with which to implement its policies. When a state starts to transform itself towards the holistic model, which means starts to manage its public property in the service to the whole, it must create the needed economic goods for its population. At this stage taxing policy is not going to the main way of procuring economic goods, but it would be supplemental. The holistic state in the face of its official representatives, but also its citizens, would have to be very precise in implementing the principles of holistic economy. Therefore, taxing policy would be used to stimulate the production and non-production of certain goods and services on its territory. As was pointed out above, the legal regime of private property in capitalistic society always generates costs for the owners in the forms of taxes and rates. Every change of the ownership and further transformation of the good leads to new taxes. The holistic governance aims to decrease the burden of the participants in the holistic organization and this includes lowering the taxes of all people in several ways:

- Logically taxes are imposed over private property. Most of the goods and services, which are provided for the participants, are public property, which have exclusive rights of usage and they should not be taxed. All movables and real estates, submitted to the participants by right and on their demand, have the purpose to satisfy the interests of the humankind and of the whole.

- The state which initiates the process of reorganization towards the holistic model aims to provide equal access to public goods for its citizens by implementing holistic economic principles of management. Holistic management of the economy is characterized with constructive distribution of the created products and it is not so much dependent on regulation of taxing burden of private property. In this way is eliminated the practice public servants to receive remuneration in the form of money which are collected from taxes. Instead, the holistic state distributes its own goods and services, created from its public property. These actions are conducted not by the selfish perspective of a ruling party or coalition of parties, but by implementing measurable practices of good governance and algorithms of protecting the equal access to public goods for all participants.

When capitalistic state collects taxes and plans the distribution of money in the annual budget, we have to stress that it does not provide directly goods and access to goods for its citizens. People remain dependent by the market and the prices of all goods and services which the merchants will ask for them. Perceiving the global market as impartial, free, or objective area on which fairness is achieved when the forces of supply and demand are meeting, is naïve, wrong and misleading statement.

The shaping of monopolies and much often oligopolistic relationships on every market is its natural condition and all well-established corporations are seeking it, because this condition guarantee higher profit, secure environment for them and prosperity. When the holistic state provides goods and services to its citizens, it is satisfying directly their needs and it is not leaving them on the favor of much stronger and selfish economic subjects in the internal or in the international trade market. Overpricing of goods, without regards whether it is basic or luxury, is performed by all corporations, because they are willing to gain from this selling. When their greed becomes unregulated by the market and by the state, the result is shrinking of the economy, lowering the access to goods for more people, social tensions, unemployment, and poorness of most people, because they do not possess economic leverage.

The new principles of holistic governance of state would eliminate the misuse of status of economic domination from private subjects or from states, which is intrinsic feature of capitalism.

Taxing policies of the holistic state may include collection of money, but they can be in the form of particular material goods. This is qualitatively different approach of stimulating of a corporation to procure specific goods, which are needed from the state. The holistic state does not need so much the money, because it is organized on different principles and its focus is to manage well its own public property. The holistic state may need specific material resources, such as a particular metal for production, technology, foods, petrol, if there is not enough renewable sources, etc. Through its taxing policy the holistic state can direct private subjects towards procuring particular goods, which is imputed on them that they owe in certain quantities for public needs. Whatever the motives of the holistic state for acquiring specific material goods, the means should be humane and respective towards the private subject. This means that taxes should not be excessively heavy for the commercial relations with private property and should not be a form of political pressure and extortion.

Apart from stimulation of specific commercial relationships, taxing policy is means for procuring of money, goods and services from external subjects with which the holistic organization has decided to develop economic relations. The motivation to impose taxes to external economic subjects which are doing business in the holistic state should also be guided by the interests of the whole. For example the collection of foreign currency would provide access to the corresponding market and with the opportunity to buy goods which are needed by the holistic organization.

The way that commercial relations with capitalistic subjects are pursuing political and ethical objectives, so are the taxing policies of the holistic state. The principles of self-sufficiency and endurance of the holistic organizations would lead to transformation of the purpose of the taxing policy of the state from main source of income to important means for economic influence over external subjects.

The role of taxing policy as a stimulus for participation in commercial relation is unnecessary and undesired in a holistic organization, because it is exploitive for a person to work in order to pay his taxes and debts, instead of working to develop himself and in service to the whole.

7. Principles of social insurance policy

Modern capitalistic states form their social insurance policies by taking money from the present work of a person, in order to provide him with future payment in the form of pension, if certain conditions are met. In this way the state has the role of distributer of the energy of the person, managing it for years and in the end is giving him something in the future. In the process of implementing this policy, there are certain factors which might leave the person with much less than it was taken from him and his access to goods might be uncertain when he is pensioner. Such factors are global financial crisis, poor management of private and public pension funds, high inflation, economic challenges in the state, high prices of goods and services and others. If social insurance contributions are not heritable and the person dies before the required age for becoming a pensioner, taking of his money from every salary was unnecessary burden which resembles a tax.

If there are not enough working people and there is senescent population in the time of his pensioning, there will be additional barriers for the state to pay decent pensions. The reason for the worldwide raising of the age for pensioning is not because there is an increase of the working performance of the people, but because the pension systems cannot bare the financial burden from an earlier pensioning.

The dependence of the pension systems from so many factors in global finances and economy, which one state is unable to control places serious risks in front of the insured people in capitalistic states.

The holistic organization is managed in the service to the whole and it has to satisfy the interests of humankind at all times. This means that it owes by right material insurance of its participants and it has to guarantee their free access to high quality and enough quantity public goods and services always. Logically this insurance continues after the time a person is obliged to work and it is due also in cases the person is not capable to work. Therefore, the age for "pensioning" (the dropping out of the obligation to work) is determined first and foremost in the interest of the person, taking into consideration his health, vitality and other factors which are relevant for his quality of life and tasks with priority. It should not be forgotten that one of the key aspects of the purpose of labor in a holistic organization is to develop the person and to bring him joy and personal satisfaction.

The estimation for discontinuing the obligation of a person to work for the holistic organization is much more comprehensive and individualized than in the capitalistic societies. The last are willing to use the person and to exploit his labor at maximum, without regards his health problems, emotional and psychological challenges and all other factors. After discontinuation of the obligation to work in a holistic organization people are eligible to contribute with their work freely, if it does not jeopardize their health and if labor brings them joy from the fact that they are integrated in the organization and they are serving to the whole.

8. Principles of insurance policy

The application of the principle of equal access to goods and services, created with public resources, would transform significantly the insurance policies which we see today in capitalistic societies. If there is an unforeseen event, which brings harm to a person or to a large group of participants of a holistic organization, including loss of public property, then a question arises: is it necessary this property to be recovered? The principle of equal access to goods means that every person and every family should be guaranteed this access at all times. If public property, distributed to a particular person, is damaged, there is a decrease of the whole property of the holistic organization. This means that the priority of the organization is to recover the access to the goods and services for the person, who is affected by the event. If the damages are more severe and cannot be recovered for a short period of time, it is necessary the burden to be shared equally by the members of the holistic organization until full recovery is reached. In this way the principle of equal access to goods will be followed and the damages would not be detrimental for particular people. This is an additional guarantee and approach to protect all participants in challenging circumstances for the organization. In capitalistic society the insurer would not guarantee the recovery, if the damages are too big. Private insurance companies are limited in their capacity to recover people and organizations in the events of large earthquakes, for example. We should never forget that insurance companies in capitalistic societies exist to exploit the fear from the insecure environment that people are living in and to profit from the fact that those fears are not always taking place in reality.

In relation to damage of a private property of a person, who is participant of a holistic organization, it is justified for it to be implemented the legal regime of insurance which is present in capitalistic society. Private owner has the right to ensure his property in private insurer. There is no legal barrier public property of a holistic organization to be insured too, if this would benefit the aims of the organization and its endurance.

There are two principal differences between the private insurer in capitalistic state and the holistic organization:

- The first difference is that the guiding motivation for the private insurer in capitalistic state is to profit from the insecurity of the people - to earn more than he recovers and to manage the money in his own interest. The private insurer does not have the purpose to maintain a protected environment, whereas the holistic organization does. Furthermore, if people are not insecure and do not fear, there would not be the need for a private insurer. This is a precondition for encouraging constant fear for the people in the system and a stimulus for ordinary people to feel alone and unprotected. The function of the holistic organization is to provide equal access to goods and services for its participants and not to profit from their insecurity. The holistic organization functions for the happiness and security of its participants and it cares for them, protects their rights and freedoms and recovers the losses for those who are suffering from the damages.

- The second principal difference is that well governed holistic organization would be much more resilient and resistant than any private insurer. If there is unforeseen event in large scale, such as strong earthquake, it is highly likely that the private insurer would bankrupt, whereas the holistic organization would mobilize all its resources for reducing the suffering, recovering all damages and sharing the burden between all participants and not only to those who are directly affected. If the private insurer company is fair, it will estimate what are the financial losses and it will recover the person with money, whereas the holistic organization is going to recover with its own labor and resources, which is much more cheap and efficient.

9. The role of money in capitalistic society

Capitalism postulates that a man should enlarge his wealth, measurable with money, in order to be successful and recognized in society and to move up the ladder of social stratification. This social raising is bringing him additional privileges, goods and services, which are intrinsic for the upper classes. It would not bring him an answer to existential questions, it would not make his labor more humane or more significant for society, but it would provide him with more things which the person is supposed to use for himself and his family.

Why managers of the capitalistic system desire to see that the main for people and organizations is to gain more money?

Money is turned to main (but not exclusive) key to access to goods and privileges for those who possess them. For central banks, printing money is an instrument for controlling the direction of the energy, which people, corporations and states produce.

In capitalistic society state institutions and independent organizations, which are taking the decisions for printing money and their entering into circulation, are interested in the actions that participants are conducting in order to gain money and not the money themselves. As the fisherman cares about the worm only as its role to be bait and not to be his meal, as central banks care about the money they print.

Every economic participant in capitalism is stimulated to gain money by finding a product which other demand and he is capable to supply. The accomplishment of this aim can be made through exercising of many diverse psychological models of acquisition of money. They can be related with selling of his labor; acquisition of property and its trade; starting a business project and exploiting the work of others; creation of the illusion of need and offering the good that is satisfying it, etc.

The common characteristic between all these psychological models, which are performed in this egoistic energetic exchange, is that they always lead to the attitude towards others as necessary means for salvation from debt and later for gaining wealth. This attitude does not allow the building of lasting and sincere harmonious relationships, because it turns all people into objects, which can potentially be used for profit. The person starts seeing himself as a tool which has to be used by someone else and for his selfish purposes. The ethical questions, related with the personal development of the individual and his spiritual needs for positive creations, are left unanswered in the background.

We should not forget that slave labor and serfdom are phenomenon which have officially existed and legal and as fundamental for the economy until the second half of XIX century. This inhumane victimization of people is the basis of capitalistic production for thousands of years. This primitive and cruel attitude towards other human-beings is forged by the driving forces of capitalism - the fear for survival, greed and desire to dominate over others.

The biggest problem which generates the social stratification, based on economic criteria, is the formation of identification of the human-being according to his property and not according to his spiritual nature and positive input for society.

When self-affirmation in society is based upon accumulation of wealth, this means that people and organizations perceive their colleagues as competitors and this is a barrier for natural cooperative efforts and common actions for solving common challenges.

The absence of internal peace and the lack of higher purpose in life lead to impossibility for harmonious inclusion in society and to blockage of the positive creative spark in the person. People, who are rising on the social ladder in capitalistic societies, often degrade as persons, if they accept the inhumane values, which the social stratification is imposing on them. Many of them starts behaving as primitive predators, which are seeking for their economic prays and not as people, who desire to solve social problems and to improve the social environment. The self-assurance that a person can "succeed" by victimizing others will always create conflicts, divisions and will maintain poverty in the system. Capitalism leads to deepening of the pathology among people, who accept domination and exploitation as necessary conditions for social prosperity.

If we compare capitalism with a jungle, inhabited by predators, where rules the principle "survival of the fittest", the managers of this system are tamers and controlling the stream of money is their "carrot" and their "stick".

Money are the main means for access to goods and services in the capitalistic society and this fact places them in the focus of economic relations between people, corporations and states. The common between all economic actors in capitalism is that they owe money to someone.

Money are also promoted as a means to freedom, indicator of dignity and worthiness and not the way they are gained, but the fact that they are possessed is valued in capitalistic society. If the working man observes his life from a higher perspective, he will easily find that he is not determining the amount of his salary, neither the prices of the goods and services he needs. The desire of every employer is to pay less and the desire of every merchant is to take more money for his products. This condition creates many unhealthy relationships among all people and dooms the social classes of constant struggle for resources and personal dislike. These attitudes are seen most clearly in crisis situation, when one group of people is taking advantage on the suffering of another.

The capitalistic system is based on a misleading postulate that goods are not enough for the needs of everyone on Earth. This statement is wrong because it equates the goods and its price in certain currency. All money which is printed out is introduced into the economy as a given credit with an interest. This means that from a global perspective the debt in money cannot be returned by all participants, because the interest is never printed and in circulation. Every additional printing means new debt and new interests. Therefore, it is irrelevant how many goods companies are producing and how many times a product is sold and made more expensive, the amount of money in circulation is not enough to return the debt. Every individual participant may try to attract money from the rest of the participants in order to return his debt and to pay the taxes to his country, but global debt cannot be returned and the system will always lack money. This lack, together with the term for pay off the debt, coerces people, corporations and countries to try to attract more money in the corresponding currency which they owe. The popular exhortation in capitalistic society "Make money!" is understood by everyone that it should not be accepted literally. No other subject, than the state or organization appointed to work as central bank, is allowed to print money. This is a prerogative and exclusive right of every state. Leading capitalistic states with disrespect to the interests of their nations had delegated the right to print money to private organizations or international structures with selfish attitudes. This places nations and political representation of the countries in huge dependence from these financial institutions which are serving the role of central banks. They are printing money with respect to their interests and those of their shareholders and not with regard to national interest or those of the global economy. "Money making" is understood as finding a way to attract or even to steal the money of others. Whether this would be compliant with legislation of a particular state or not depends entirely the ethics of the person or of the organization. Whether law would be enforced depends on the corresponding state organs. In conclusion we can point out that money and not material goods are artificially limited resource, which is due in a larger amount that actually exists.

What is the difference of debt in money and debt in reproducible economic goods?

Let's hypothetically imagine that a state desires to stimulate its population to produce specific material goods and it lends credit of tomatoes seeds with interest in tomatoes for one person, cherry trees with interest in cherries for another person, hens with interest in eggs for a third one. All these material goods have something in common and it is that they can be reproduced and new goods can be created from them. This means that if there is good governance from the debtor, he could return his credit with the interests and at the same time he will be able to use the other items for himself without being necessary for him to take something from another person.

Therefore, the problem of the interest rate of money is not so much related with the desire of the creditor to profit, but with the inability of all debtors to return their debt, because there is not enough money in circulation. This inability leads to worsening the relationships between participants in capitalistic society, because some of them are always going to declare their bankruptcy unless they do not receive the benevolence of their creditors and their debt is not forgiven or postponed. Financial dependence of states always leads to a political one.

We can illustrate that the financial system in capitalistic society is built on similar principles of a popular children's game "Musical chairs" in which several children are circling around chairs on the background of music. With sudden stop of the music every child should find a chair to sit and it happens so that the chairs are one less than the children. The child, who did not manage to sit, is eliminated from the game. For the rest the music starts again and they are up and circling and singing. On every continuation a chair is removed and always one person will not be able to sit, when the music stops. The winner is the child which has remained the last on the last chair.

In this metaphor the children are economic subjects such as people, corporations and states, the circling around the chairs, clapping of their hands and singing represents the economic relationships, whereas the sitting is the debt that they have to return to the creditors. The person who is playing and stopping the music is the central bank institution.

In the end in this game conditional winner is only one of the children and all others are losers on a different time frame. Precisely this is proposing the financial system in capitalism.

10. Application of the holistic economy

How to apply in practice the holistic approach for creation of a working economy, which is capable to satisfy the interests of the whole?

Capitalistic economy is capable to function by limiting the access to all goods and services and their provision against the completion of a specific task. The pressure from this limitation motivates the people to overcome this unpleasant situation and to do what is expected from them and for what they are going to be paid. The dependent subject (an employee or a debtor) agrees his behavior to be guided by the controlling subject - employer or creditor. This guidance does not necessarily bring more satisfactory results for the whole and for all other subjects, because its purpose is to bring energy for the subject on the top of the economic chain of dependence.

The holistic economy does not rely on limitations and deprivations in order to motivate the people to perform certain tasks. It uses the approach of provision of all necessary goods from public resources, which are set for equal distribution to all participants. The provision of goods is always on the time of occurrence of the need and it is not intermediated by currency or credit from a bank. If a person disrespects the values of the holistic organizations and violates the rules, which he has declared to comply with, the reaction of the holistic organization should not be to punish him by limiting his access to goods, but to implement humane measures of restoring the behavior of the person. If he is not willing to live by the rules of the holistic society, the person is respectfully relived from duty and cast out from the organization.

Logically the question arises: what will motivate the people to create different goods and services? The holistic organization should develop its own capacity to create and provide all goods and services which are vital for the people and needed by them. It is prudent the holistic organization to start from a product which is needed by everyone, important for the development of all people and for the environment. An example of such product is the house of a participant of the holistic organization.

Even in modern day capitalistic societies it can be initiated the implementation of the holistic approach towards the economy.

Besides remuneration with money, the state or private organization, which are willing to adopt the holistic approach, may build and provide the lodging that the people need. Against this, a person is obliged to participate in the working process with a profession, beneficial to the whole, which is available and which he possesses the skills and knowledge to practice.

The practicing of this profession is for a period of time, which the organization determines, but the term is regarding the physical and psychological capabilities of the person and the objective is not to exploit him as much as possible. An example of such maximum period of time for compulsory practice of a profession is thirty years. After the completion of this period, the person is free to choose whether to continue working, if he desires so. Without regards his choice, he will be able to receive all types of goods and services, which are available for all other participants until the end of his life. Except the house, all other goods and services, created from public resources, are provided as a form of right to the person, according to the principles, reviewed above. These products are made by all participants of the holistic organization, who have also received their lodging from the community. People, who are directly engaged with the construction of all houses, apartments and other buildings, would also receive their needed home with an agreement to participate in the construction process for the next thirty years. The material resources, which are going to be used for the buildings are public property, which is set for this purpose. In this way is powered the economic wheel in a direction, which is desired by the people and by the organization. Through the provision of the home, which the person desires, the organization satisfies one of the most important of his basic needs immediately and without being necessary for him to enter into debt to a bank. This means that this person doesn't have to satisfy the greed of the construction company, merchants and banks in order to have a lodging. The direct provision of a home with high quality for the participant, who agrees to perform his working duties forms a strong bond between the person and the organization, which cannot be affected by financial speculations, devaluation of a currency, raising of interest rates from a bank, financial speculation, poor economic performance, unemployment, raising of the prices of the real estate, lowering the remuneration and others.

In order to illustrate this form of payment, it can be presented in numbers, as the mechanisms of the capitalistic system are working. They are conditional and serve as an example. If an employer, including a state, in a well-developed capitalistic society pays to his employee a salary of 2000 currency units and for the buying of a decent home are needed 100,000 of the same currency units, then for the employee most often there would be a lack of funding to buy his home. He is forced to look for a bank credit. Let's assume that the conditions of the bank are favorable and it offers him a credit with fixed interest rates of 5 % and 100 % of funding of his home for the next 30 years. The result is that the debtor will have to pay almost twice the price of his home and he will spend from his salary 530 units in the next three decades. Even more, his employer will have to find money for his salary and indirectly he is the one, who is paying the credit and profit of the construction company and the profit of all other intermediaries on the chain and the increased taxes from the expenses. In a well-functioning market, in which everyone is prescient to limit the amount of his profit in reasonable volume, the costs of the construction company of this house would be around 40,000 of these currency units. Consequently, the employee, even in this most beneficial case, where he is not fired, healthy and for 30 years there is no economic crisis, would have to pay 5 times the price of his home. The employer would have to provide 5 times more money to the salary of his employee and their only advantage is that they have 30 years to do that. In this classical example of economic functioning, the energy of the employer is spent for the payment of the desired profit of construction companies, banks and intermediaries for all his staff, who are buying their homes. Those economic actors are exploiting indirectly the employer and they are capable to do that, because the employees are unable to satisfy their needs of homes immediately.

In an ill functioning capitalistic state, such as Bulgaria, the greed of the economic actors on the chain is much larger and the sources of income much limited. In these countries the salaries would be 1000 currency units, the price of a decent home would be 120,000 and the credit from a bank would be 7 % for a period of 30 years. In this case the lodging of the person would cost 280,000 which are 7 times more than the costs of its construction and the monthly bank installment would be ¾ of the salary of the employee. Therefore, the employer is practically paying most of his costs for banking interest and for the greed of the construction company in order to provide for the need of home of his employee.

What would happen if an employer and an employee apply partially the holistic approach and form much stronger relationships of trust towards each other and change the economic chain, by cutting the other economic subjects, their service and profit? This change can happen, if the employer substitutes the role of the investor in real estates (or construction company), who is building the house for the employee for 40,000 currency units. Then the employer easily substitutes the bank and its service of credit by providing the house/apartment to his employee as part of his salary. If the employer is not capable to use funds from his own company, he may take a credit for the sum of construction for a period of 30 years. In case of 7 % annual interest, he would have to pay the bank 260 units every month and the total sum would be 94,000 currency units. Therefore, the employer will lighten significantly his own costs for salary of the employee and he will release his employee of dependence from the bank, which exists in the classical capitalistic model of currency flow. The formed relationships between employer and employee are going to be much stronger and lasting than they are in the first scenario.

If we go back to the ideal holistic model, we can trace the positive outcomes from a holistic organization to be responsible for the construction of the homes of its participants.

Firstly, it will be able to build all houses or apartments by overall planning of their location, with innovative ecological materials and systems, with care of their efficient heating, water supply, decreasing of oil imprint, or dependence on gas. Larger scales of this project could lead to significant lowering of the costs than in individual initiating from every participant. The quality of the lodging would be much better, because the pressure of the market to lower the costs would not exist. The consumers are the participants and there is no competition with other construction companies, because the provision of house resembles a form of payment. In order to be free and sustainable in its development, the holistic organization should focus on usage of renewable sources of energy and avoiding petroleum and gas products. For example, if there are good conditions for using the energy of the Sun, or the wind for the residence and production needs of the holistic organization, it would be achieved the objective of independence from corporations and states, which are providing oil and gas.

The second positive effect from the construction of real estate, without searching profit from a fast sale, is that the houses and other buildings could be optimally spacious and high quality architectural creations. At the same time they could be constructed in a way to satisfy the individual needs and desires of every participant.

The holistic organization would determine what the resources are to ensure with residential area all its participants. This residential area would have to be by all means qualitative enough for good family planning. The homes of participants in a holistic organization are going to be better than those of representatives of the middle class of well-developed capitalistic society.

The third positive effect from this endeavor is related with the possibility of the participant to choose the location of his home, its composition and architectures, the space of his rooms and all other individual characteristics that could make his home a unique expression of his character and which would not be a serious effort for the holistic organization. This freedom is not typical for the capitalistic and communistic societies in which most of the people, who are capable to buy family house, are choosing between very narrow diversity of houses or apartments.

Another positive effect from the global planning of the residential construction is the possibility for provision of high quality services for common use. Such may be pools, sporting center, tennis courts, playgrounds, parks, gardens, rooms for artistic activities and performances, exhibit halls, seminar rooms and all other specialized areas that the participants are willing to have.

One of the most important positive effects from the construction and provision of a house to the participant is the forming of a strong relationship between the person and the organization, which is not intermediated by currency and therefore cannot be attacked with financial speculations, caused in the global financial market thousands of kilometers away.

The end result of this organization of the residential area and homes is satisfied interest of the participants, because they are going to live in qualitatively build ecological homes, which they desire. Next, it is satisfied the interest of the holistic organization of having secured its participants with one of their most important basic needs and stimulated them to work and create for it additional products. At the same time is satisfied the interest of Earth, because are used the best ecological materials, systems, methods and techniques of construction. In the process of construction are respected also the interests of animals and plants.

CHAPTER 6

LABOR RELATIONS IN A HOLISTIC ORGANIZATION

Labor has many functions in society. The remuneration for a working position is an indicator for the attitudes of the community towards different professions and different participants. From the way labor relations are structured, we can understand what the principles are for using planetary resources and for distributing the goods and services to people. It is precisely the intention of various groups of people to wide their labor rights what caused the most significant social revolutions and it is precisely the provision of those rights what caused the more humane development of the civilization. The provision of labor rights also leads to economic development.

These processes are especially intensive in the struggle of elimination of slavery. It is yearning of freedom and substitution of one form of economic relations with more humane and just - those of free provision of labor force for payment. Later, the bad conditions of the workers, their low payment and the practice of exploiting children had brought massive protests and organized social movements to introduce safety rules and decent wages. The next cause - the defense of the rights of the women for equal payment and equal access to the labor market had resulted in much more balance society in all aspects of relations between the two genders. Strong standing for these causes continues to be an important pillar of the humanity of our civilization.

The attitude towards labor and the role of the state for the labor market are main ideological differentiation lines between right and left political movements and schools of thought. It should be reminded that both political families belong to egoistic models of social order, because they are defending one-sidedly the interests of different classes of society. Main criterion for their differentiation is the understanding for the level of protection of the rights of the workers and all employees.

The holistic view for policy and economics regard the positive aspects and strong thesis of both political ideologies from the perspective of the service to the whole, but it far above them in relation to perspective, aim, management and methods.

The holistic economy has one purpose - to propose holistic vision for the implementation of socio-political projects, which are satisfying in the best possible way the interests of the subjects of the holistic model.

Capitalistic economy functions by separating people in classes and enriching appointed elite groups of the population, who have usurped the right to choose and to legally determine what access to goods all people are going to have.

The role of labor in capitalistic society is clearly set in the international labor law and national legislation of all countries. Similar principles are adopted in the Western societies and in some of the developing nations. However, in different parts of the world are proclaimed very different labor rights, which are conditioned by cultural, religious and economic specifics of different nations. Human labor still is the main resource for the global economy. In the XX century the International Labor Organization in the UN system of specialized agencies adopted series of international standards, basic principles and rights to conduct labor. However, the negative phenomena of slavery, forced labor, child labor, discrimination on the working place, insignificant remuneration are still ongoing with no evidence whatsoever of their elimination. Zero tolerance towards these inhumane phenomena historically and until today is the strongest beacon of light which helps humanity free itself chain by chain. The violation of labor rights always represents a violation of the interests of the humankind. The legal adoption of more rights for the people is a form of acknowledgement that humankind stands above all nations and all corporations.

Humanization of the labor relations is an important part of the holistic organization of the working process, but it is not the only direction of necessary change.

Despite the progress of the civilization in its views for the human labor and the partial not very effective bans and attempts to eliminate the above mentioned forms of violation of human rights, there is no country or corporation which had reached the ideal theoretical humanistic point of view about how human labor should be inspired and managed. Furthermore, presently there is not a single country which had formed clearly this ideal and set the goal of reaching it. The reason is that for states and corporations humans are important only as a resource for their survival. More prescient managers know that this resource has to be developed, inspired and rewarded and they are taking care of those humans, who can produce something valuable for them. Despite the good care, these managers are also seeing humans predominantly as needed parts of a mechanism, without which the prosperity of their organization is impossible. The introduction of artificial intelligence and robots in capitalistic production will prove this thesis, because capitalistic countries will refuse to take care of the people, because they are not so useful anymore.

The modern capitalistic system had identified several important functions of human labor, which are different for the three key actors in working relations - the employee, the private employer and the state as a regulator. It is correct to perceive the state as a regulator on one side, but also as a top employer in key spheres of society.

Labor has different purpose for the three actors. For the employee it is a key means for access to goods and survival, as well as for rising on the ladder of classes in capitalism. Human labor gives an opportunity for the employee to buy a house, raise a family, immerse in different cultures, gain knowledge and all other form of development and joy that he is able to experience. However, many working people have chosen their job, because they want to be of service to other people and to society in general in a specific way and not just for earning more money and get more privileges. For them the remuneration and social status are not the driving force of choosing a particular job and they will not be the decisive factor of changing it. For them the most important thing is what they give to humanity and not what does the capitalistic system gives in return. The implicit coercion to take a job, which the corporation or the state offers and not the one that the person strives from within in order to be useful for the community or to achieve mastery in a desired field is one of the greatest problems in the organization of the contemporary labor relations. This problem is theoretically solved in the holistic economy.

From the perspective of the corporation human labor is means for survival and growth and humans are a resource for gaining advantage over competitors. For this reason the corporation is supporting those types of character and knowledge development in its employees, which will help the company being stronger and more competitive. The private employer is not responsible to encourage this development which will be most needed and desired by the person. Generally, most of the corporations do not have a focus and they do not care very much whether their goods and services are produced in the interests of humankind and the whole, because they are functioning in a highly competitive environment and survival is the priority. As it is well known many corporations exploit people in very disrespectful manner to humankind. This form of corporate management hinders social development of the people and blocks many of their functions and social roles such as being a parent, husband, friend, researched, spiritual seeker, sports lover, etc. Corporations in most cases desire to use a human-being as much as they can and many of them organize the working process and environment to be very obsessive. These methods create serious misbalance between the work and the other social functions that a person has. These working relations blind the people about the interests of humankind and those of the whole.

The second huge problem which is generated, because of the perspective of the private corporation is that the created products do not always serve humanity and their usage very often is even in its detriment. Examples of such goods are all types of weapons for massive destruction, unhealthy foods, cigarettes, etc. There are many other goods and services which are not useful for the people and at least should not be with priority over other more useful goods in relation to usage of resources and directing human energy and talent.

From the perspective of the modern state it is not very important for the governmental officials what the type of labor of an employee is in a private corporation.

Every state is interested in the statistical date of employment, economic and financial results, but not so much whether the goods are produced with optimal resources and whether the goods are in the interest of humankind. The state is not interested in the level of personal development from the conducting of specific work. The focus of all states in relation to production is selfishly oriented. For example innovation of technological equipment, which can be used to gain strategic advantage over a competitor or an enemy state would be funded with priority over civil production, even when a there is not an immediate security threat.

We can conclude that the capitalistic system focuses the attention of all three actors (employee, private employer and state) on what they can get in exchange of the production and not over the significance and application of the created goods and services. This leads to deformation of all relations between people, an attitude of managed mutual exploitation and in the end- inhumane treatment of people, environmentally unfriendly usage of Earth and its resources and harsh violations of the interests of animals and plants. The maintenance of this type of labor relation creates a social picture which is not in the service to the whole.

What is holistic management of labor?

All human-beings possess many social roles which good performance is crucial for their personal development, but also for the development of humankind. Holistic management of labor means building harmonious relationships between the person with all his social roles and the system, so that they both serve the interests of the whole. The labor, which every person conducts, should be regarded with all other activities that are important for the person to conduct in his free time. This means that the working position is structured in a way to develop the person and to protect his rights individually for everyone.

Except individual synchronization, holistic management of labor includes also interconnection between different economic and social fields, so that all activities are serving optimally the interests of the whole. To achieve this complex task, the holistic management needs to make and use thorough in-depth analysis of different sectors of the economy and to determine the most efficient ways of satisfying the interests of the whole.

The capitalistic system gives rise to corporate greed, which is the result of unstoppable competition, whereas the holistic system supports the emergence of organizations which are working in synchronization as the organs of a living organism. This new form of governance aims to achieve voluntary integration between private and public subjects in this case - the holistic state. It is mandatory this integration to be voluntary, otherwise the holistic model would become another dictatorship under beautiful slogans! This means that private organization have always to be free to make the initiative to become one with a holistic state and to provide their resources to be used in the service to the whole. This inevitably would lead to transformation of all production processes, increasing of the quality of goods and services, widening of the scope of their users, changing the ways of acquiring and manage all resources, lowering mandatory working time and many other components. To trace the transition from capitalistic to holistic systems, we will have to review the specifics of labor relations in a holistic organization.

The management of every holistic organization would require overall planning of the economy, before a job position is created, than any other private organization or state have done in the past. For a modern corporation it is important to know what are the attitudes, needs and desires of its target group of customers; how to influence them and to understand what is the market influenced by in the respective sector. For the holistic organization, on the other hand, is needed much more diverse information of the whole environment which is shown briefly below.

One of the most important characteristics of the holistic labor process is that in the system are not encouraged competitive relations between all participants and different institutions and departments. The opportunity for a free market with private goods is preserved for those people, who are willing to profit, but it would not be the only option of access to needed goods and services as it is in capitalism. Because of the fact that the holistic organization is going to provide public goods and services for free as a form of due right, in the internal relations would be naturally eliminated the classical capitalistic understanding of trade deals between a merchant and a consumer. The internal relations between participants in the holistic organization, related to the production and provision of goods, are turning money into unnecessary means for payment. The absence of a convertible currency, which could be affected by global manipulations of the market and by financial crises, provides an opportunity for the holistic organization to be conserved, resilient and stable economic subject which is in control of its resources and their distribution at all times. The holistic organization would become immune from negative foreign influence of the world financial markets where everyone is in competition. Huge challenge in front of every small holistic organization would be to provide variety of goods on demand for its participants. Parts of its own public resources the holistic organizations may trade with external subjects if from these commercial activities would benefit the whole, as was already pointed out in chapter five.

In the developed stage of application of the holistic labor process is absent remuneration of the employees for their working activities and the wage is completely replaced with free access to huge variety of goods and services, created from public resources. This access is equal as quality with those of all other participants and this would change entirely the motivation of a person to work comparing to those that are maintained in the capitalistic state. The substitution of financial payment with real direct access to public goods and services would eliminate the consequences of the speculative trade and constantly increasing prices for every product. People would be able use much more goods and services, because the cost of the greed of every merchant on the chain would not be included as energy that somebody has to deliver.

In the process of forming job description should be included the qualities that the person should develop during the period of time he is working. In addition to the written requirements of the employee's duties, he would have the right to know how are going to be used the results of his work. Such right does not exist in a capitalistic corporation.

1. Type of labor

In the process of reviewing the holistic production process, we have established that all created goods and provided services should be useful for the whole. This means that the activities, that the employee is conducting and their results should bring him much more satisfaction than the labor in capitalistic system. It is because many of the modern jobs are not designed to develop significantly the working individuals. At the same time many professions are not oriented towards biodiversity and protection of Earth's resources.

When the labor of a person is useful for the whole and the access to quality goods and services is sufficient and equal to that of all other participants, it is highly likely that a person is going to focus much more on what he would like to give, create and provide for the people, instead of estimating the money he is receiving from them. Lowering the levels of personal insecurity, fear for survival and greed would contribute significantly to drawing the attention of people on the needs of the society. This fundamental change of the focus would open the doors for more creativity in the working process, which is going to be directed in the best possible way for the society, instead of the best possible way for the stakeholders as it is today. Another positive outcome would be the building of meaningful and complete relationship between people, who are directly involved in an activity.

The notion that we do something in order to guarantee our own survival and prosperity is replaced by the feeling that we are really working for the community and for the whole. The goods and services we would receive as a due human right and not as a form of reward.

Next, the labor should be much safer and the health of the employee protected, than it is foreseen in modern developed capitalistic societies. The example of the workers in the chicken factory is very illustrative that the health and the safety measures in these working places are not sufficient and much more can be done. The safety conditions on the working place are not a priority in the modern labor process, especially in the developing countries.

The holistic management of the labor process includes the creation of job positions, which are much safer and which are not threatening the health of the employees. If activity or job positions are dangerous for the health of the employees, but they are absolutely necessary for the holistic organization, much more safety measures have to be taken by the management to reduce the level of threat to the health as much as possible. These measures have to be determined thoroughly for all job positions and working activities.

With the development of the holistic system the working conditions for all people would have to reach a stage when they are not harmful for the people, but they are very useful for their personal development.

How to motivate a person to take a job position, which includes the conducting of hard and unpleasant labor?

Every economic system includes working activities, which are not especially pleasant and desired by most people and arises the question: who is going to conduct them and how to motivate the people, if the organization provides the same access to goods and services for every job? Before giving the answer, let's make a brief overview how developed capitalistic societies are solving this problem. If we take for example the activity of cleaning of a smeary factory or conducting all other type of hard physical labor, which is dangerous and in unhealthy environment and that does not require higher education.

In all developed capitalistic societies such activities are conducted by people, who are comparatively low educated, most of them represent marginalized ethnic minority, or are immigrants. These types of work are performed whole day, usually starting in the lower hours of the day. For cleaning activities is paid the minimum wage. Despite that it is not required to have a higher education the need of this job for society is undisputed. If a university is closed and stops functioning the results from the absence of qualified and educated people would be felt after years, but if a city is not cleaned for a week, the whole system will be paralyzed. Therefore, in order these positions to be permanently occupied, the capitalistic system finds a way to maintain low levels of education among large groups of its society and creates an environment in which these people do not have other choice. The most widely used way of filling these job positions is by letting immigrants (including illegal ones), who are looking for salvation from their even lower developed society. By including illegal immigrants in the economy, the capitalistic states are capable to exploit them for many years and to pay them the low wages. This form of employment is much closer to slavery and violates human rights, than to a profession which provides freedom for further development of the person. The choice of conducting hard physical labor is made by people, who prefer the lesser evil than poverty and human rights violation in their own states.

The holistic approach foresees the formation of much healthier labor conditions than are foreseen in capitalism. It includes strengthening of the automation of the activities, especially those which are not developing enough the personal and social skills of the employee and are not desired by people. The next important element is decreasing of the working time for necessary, but not desired professions. This would lead to contracting more people for these positions, but for a shorter period of time. The decreasing of time would not lead to lower access to goods and services, which is logical in relation to applying the principal of equality in this sense for the participants in the organization.

2. Type of job positions

The management of the larger part of the economic processes in a holistic society and its direction towards satisfying the needs of humankind and the interests of the whole would lead to significant structural transformation of the number and of the types of job positions. This is a logical result from the elimination of competition between different corporations and the optimization of human labor and resources. The requirement every job position to be regarded with the interests of the whole would change the focus to professions in the areas of social activities, education, ecology, science, architecture, art instead of banking, finances and those related with increasing of the demand of products and of the profits of the private organizations.

Another important requirement for the creation of every job position is to be at the same time needed for the holistic system and desired by the employees. This is a crucial difference with the capitalistic economic environment which compels people to look for a job on the market and not being able to remodel the position together with the employer.

The holistic system frees itself from the motivation forces of applying for job to be greed and fear for personal survival. For a holistic organization it is important to create attractive professional positions, which are individually shaped for the people, who are going to fill them. Main function of the job positions is to develop the person in direction of service to the whole.

Presently, many people are compelled to have a job which is not satisfying them, because the economic environment and their present skills and attitudes are such that they are not capable to find a decent alternative.

From a holistic point of view it would be extremely poor decision to create a job position in which you place a person in 5 square meters to sell tickets and at the same time to have a machine next to him which is performing the same activity. The people, who are having these jobs nowadays, are making a living in an honest and lawful way and the criticism of the system is not at all personally addressed to them.

The holistic society aims to provide the opportunities for everyone to find the suitable form of self-expression with a profession with which he is useful to the whole. In every community exists the need of conducting activities which are not very pleasant and which might be dangerous for the person and his health. The holistic management of the labor process is guided by the principles of lowering the unpleasant sides of an activity; reducing the compulsory working time for it; introduction of machines which can substitute the person, or at least support him with his activities; taking optimal measures for protecting his health, etc. These principles are in sharp contrast with capitalistic societies, which are solving the problem of conducting unpleasant work by maintaining ineffective educational and social systems; by limiting the access of goods to large groups; by letting immigrants in their countries in order to have these jobs.

The holistic society has clear aim and long-term goals of evolution which include personal development of its own participants. Job positions in the system are main instrument for achieving quality life, individual and collective professional mastery. The job positions in a holistic organization should be created in regards to each other. A position should serve as a preparation for another one and the skills that employee acquires in the first are those that are needed in the second.

3. Right to be informed about the results from the labor

The holistic management of the labor process includes also the right of the employee to be informed about the results from his labor. This means that the participant should have access to information for what purpose will be used the added value from his activities and from the project he is part of. At first glance it may seem that this right exists also today in capitalistic system, but this is not true. The corporations do not owe to their employees to give them information about the working process, the impact from the products and how is the income of the company budgeted. The employees in a typical capitalistic corporation are not aware of the overall impact of the organization and of the conclusions and recommendations in audit reports of the company or its contractors. This is omission of ethical synchronization between an employer and employee in capitalism.

In the holistic system every participant has the right to know all aspects of the impact of the organization and he is encouraged to exercise it. This information is a needed for the participant in order to determine how well is protected the interest of the whole and to be aware of the importance of his work and those of his colleagues. The participants are going to see themselves as part of a chain which creates an organization with positive impact on many levels. The freedom of a participant to be included in the social activities can be guaranteed only if he receives enough information of the results and impact from them.

Because the access to public goods is the same for all participants/ employees in the holistic system and the focus of attention in labor is on the following questions: What we do? How we do it? What needs are we satisfying? How well we distribute the products? For this reason the need to know the process and the impact from the labor is much bigger than in capitalistic society.

Every labor activity can be perfected more, so that it harms the planet less. The person, who has reached ecological awareness, cannot easily ignore the fact that his working activities do harm to humans, Earth, animals, or trees. Through the provision of access to information for all stages of the economic process, the holistic system gives an opportunity for the person to participate globally in various projects and to express his desire for positive impact through his work. From management point of view the motivation for participation and inspiration for positive impact are driven through the provision of truthful information about the labor process. This is main stimulus in the holistic system. In order to drive the economic wheel in a holistic society, it is necessary to encourage the participants to raise their awareness.

Capitalistic society on the contrary to the holistic one needs employees, who are not asking questions about the impact of the organization, the effect of their labor and generally people are easily stimulated by egoistic means.

4. Right to address proposals for change of the management of the labor process

The holistic system by definition is in process of permanent improvement with regards to the activities for satisfaction of the whole.

The provision of sufficient information to the participants about the functioning of the holistic organization is bound with the possibility everyone to make motivated proposals for change and with the obligation of the organization to consider the ideas.

The holistic approach sees every participant as a manifestation of the Absolute and part of the whole. Because of that people are capable of unique observations and visions of the development of the organization. Therefore, it is needed that the organization is open to listen and welcomes motivated proposals for development. The community stimulates its participants to pay attention to what they do and to think of ways to improve the process and to integrate different policies. When the attention of the employees is focused on the quality of their labor and the direct and indirect effects from it, they would develop much more creative approach to improve the holistic system than they are able to improve capitalistic system.

The modern day egoistic system relies on management which resembles control and not facilitation of positive creative initiatives. We can see that in the efforts of different corporations and governmental entities to hide the true nature of their influence. The egoistic system often needs to block the development of its people, especially in relation to understanding the results of their activities. In capitalism is ruling the mentality to execute without thinking and to act without asking questions or provide better alternatives. In order for capitalistic system be successfully applied, it is necessary the rulers to block the development of attitudes like constructive thinking about the nature of the system, desires for cooperation, balanced consumption, striving for higher personal and social ethics. Imperative governance is much harder to be implemented when for the people is created an environment of real freedom, critical thinking, positive creative actions, access to goods by right, and all of these aspects combined to be in service to the whole. The reason is that well-grounded demands for improvement emerge and they are putting the system on the road of inevitable positive transformation. This is a process which would lead to weakening of its harsh methods for influence and control by maintaining different levels of limitations and lack for everyone.

The holistic system needs the grounded proposals of its participants in order to be improved and it has to create the conditions for them to form and address them to the management. It is precisely the arguments of a proposal and the rationales for better satisfaction of the interests of the whole are the relevant criteria whether to adopt it. In egoistic systems the criteria to adopt a proposal are the number of people, who have signed behind it, the official position of the person or the group of people, who are making it.

For the participants of a holistic organization it should be crystal clear that some of the best proposals can be made from everyone and also that some of the most harmful proposals can be made by people, who are at high-level positions and who are responsible for large groups of people. If the last happens, this is a sign that the organization requires improvement in the career development of its employees and of the early identifications of the ethics of its members.

The egoistic system, on the other side, is much rigid and resists positive transformation, because the higher ideal in this system is the survival on the accounts of the others. Power is turned as a prize for those, who are seeking most this surviving and for those who are craving social approval. This leads to disrespect of the interest of the whole and placing the focus towards internal political and corporate rivalry, instead of nourishing harmony in the environment. The egoistic systems are always imperative and imposing, whereas the holistic - free and contracting. This difference is highlighting which system develops its participants and which one is merely exploiting them.

5. Determining of the duration of the working time

When the employer is a holistic organization, it has to regard the free time of his employees and to appreciate it as their necessity to live, to develop themselves and to be happy. People in a holistic system are free to choose how to spend their free time and the holistic approach towards labor management includes creating of a job position which does not jeopardize the other activities of the person, which are important for him. The main difference between holistic and capitalistic systems is that in the last the free time serves mainly for recovery of the strength of the person, whereas in the holistic one its purpose is appreciated as additional time for development of the person in a direction, chosen by him.

The egoistic organizations are not interested very much whether their employees have enough time for desired social contacts, individual activities, relaxation, or outside office duties. For them it is not important, if a person needs more time to sleep, additional time for meditation, more time to communicate with his family, or to overcome psychological issue. Egoistic organizations' main purpose is to use the employee and to be as much vital and recovered for the next working day to provide his labor and talents. Paradoxically in capitalistic system, corporations and states "drain" the maximum the energy in the form of labor from their participants, but at the same time waste it for the production of products which are not optimal quality and quantity.

In the last half century we are witnessing unprecedented technological development of the society, scientific discoveries, three-time increase of the working force, and globalization of the economy. All these positive results have not led to increase of the welfare of most of the people, neither to mitigation of their labor or decreasing of their working time. The reason is because capitalistic states maintain scarcity and limitation for people and those from lower classes are always on the edge of survival. Capitalism shall always maintain low income for the majority of the population and it will always put limitations to higher education for most of them in order to guarantee fulfillment of its lower rank positions. Capitalistic system is unpleasant and unwelcome also for representatives of lower and higher management, who are forced to maintain the model despite, that they do not share its goals, methods and outcomes. The professional commitment in the egoistic systems includes most of the time of all working people. For capitalism the production is stimulated by the driving force of service to self. It is driven by greed and free time is considered as "necessary evil" for recovery of the people and not a desired outcome of the managers of the capitalistic system.

The holistic system, on the other hand, foresees planning of its own production on the basis of the real needs of the people and the capabilities of Earth. Therefore, the production and other stages of the holistic economy have end result, parameters for enough production in quantity and in quality, after which additional work is not needed by people. Overproduction is undesired phenomenon in the holistic system and if it occurs, this is an indicator for poor management and disharmony of the processes. The global way of organizing the labor would provide an opportunity for optimal effective direction of the results from it in order to be satisfied the interests of the whole. Therefore, the compulsory working time of the employees should be decreased when it is possible!

The principles for determining of the duration of the compulsory working time in the holistic system are two:

• The first principle is to determine how much labor force is needed and to divide it by hours (man-hours) in order to achieve the objectives of the organization. When are discovered or introduced new management practices and innovations, which are capable to organize the labor process in such a way, so that the objectives are achieved for a lower working time, the compulsory working time should be decreased. The increase of the number of employees in the holistic organization and the improvement of their working relationships would also lead to achieving the objectives for a less time. When an economic subject aims to achieve optimal production and avoidance of unneeded products, every type of improvement of the labor process would lead to mitigation of the general obligations and reducing the working time for the employees.

• The second principle for determining of the duration of the working time is related with the interests of the employee. The holistic organization is not a prison for the participants in which they have to find a way to survive, but it aims to provide them with more pleasant and more joyful environment in which people are having time for various form of positive self-expression, entertainment and creative projects. Holistic society aims to provide enough free time for all of its participants, so that they could be able to choose freely direction of development.

In the holistic organization there are two types of labor: basic and additional.

The basic labor is the one that is needed for the organization to achieve its set objectives and economic goals. It is estimated in man-hours and it has to be equally distributed for all participants. The maximum duration should not exceed six hours per day, because this would deprive the employee from enough free time. Every participant is entering into his contract with the holistic organization and in it are stipulated the parameters of basic labor, which he is obliged to perform. Essentially this is a labor contract, but as it was already pointed out, between the two sides are additional requirements and obligations. The relations between a holistic organization and its participant are much more integrated than they are between an employer and employee in the classical labor relationship.

Every labor, which a person is conducting in addition to his compulsory one, is called additional. The additional labor is performed voluntarily and it cannot be demanded from the employee as his duty. Those activities can be in his contracted professional area or in another field, which the person desires to be part of. The employee is free to work in areas which are not with priority of the organization to place human labor and resources. The person, who is willing to perform additional labor may also wish to speed up a working process and invest more of his time on the same project which he is part of in his compulsory time to satisfy faster the needs of the participants. There is no prohibition whatsoever the person to conduct additional labor outside the holistic organization, if his work is legal and it is not violating the interests of the whole.

The additional labor in a holistic organization does not bring the person more goods and services, but it is an indicator of his dedication and commitment to the organization and the interests of the community. The performing of additional labor cannot be allowed if it harms the person's health. In order to perform his desired additional labor, the person has to receive certain resources, which are not difficult to be distributed by the organization. The holistic organization is responsible for the provision of these resources and it has to do everything in its capacity to facilitate the implementation of the project of the participant. Such needed resources can be office space, consumables, electronics, access to library, statistical data, network of like-minded people, etc.

If the holistic organization is managed well, the compulsory working time can be reduced and become even less than six hours per day. The holistic labor management includes both compulsory and additional labor. The criteria for determining both types is whether the person is working on the basis of contract with the holistic organization, or he is willing to contribute his labor and talents to improve the organization. It is important for the holistic organization what motivation is driving the person to work and to what extent it can rely on him for defending the interests of the whole.

The freely conducted additional labor is a form of responsibility towards the community and not a legal obligation to the organization. It signifies the development of free individuals in a holistic society. It is not enough one activity to be optimized and to be useful for the society. It is much better, if this activity is less and less compulsory until the society is confident that the participant would freely organize to serve the interests of the whole. In order to reach this level of attitude, it is necessary that people have built ethics in service to the whole and have confidence in the system and in the participants in the organization. Only then the ideal of holistic society is reached.

If people do not desire to conduct freely their labor, the holistic organization is not forcing, judging or punishing them. Equal access to goods and services remains unchanged for all, as it is supposed to be written in their contracts with the holistic organization. The freely donated labor is an indicator of the will of the participants to develop the holistic organization. It is a representation of the fact that people are choosing their roles in the community freely and that they are willing to live in service to the whole. Through the stepwise and precisely organized introduction of the free additional labor, would be reached a significant shift of perception about the responsibility that people do take to develop their society.

6. Individual determination of the job position

In order to find a balance between the interests of the holistic organization and the employee, it is necessary the labor contract to be individualized according to the needs of both the community and the person. As an employer, which is planning in large scale its development, the holistic organization has a leading role in determination of the job description. It chooses the type of activity, which is needed to be performed and the location for conducting them. It is impossible to provide additional payment, privileges or different access to goods and services to the employees, because this will be in complete violation of the principle of equal access to public goods. This principle is one of the fundaments of building holistic society. The holistic organization provides an opportunity for the employee to practice a profession of his own choice in a larger and larger variety of possible positions, depending on his skills and knowledge. The difference between the competitions for professional positions in capitalistic society and in a holistic one is that in the last the holistic organization aims to satisfies the desires of the people to work specific job in the best possible way. It also aims to make the working place as pleasant as possible and to be a stepping stone and main instrument for the personal development of the employee. The individualization of the contract of the employee aims to turn the profession of the employee as fulfilling his professional dream. The job position in a holistic organization is designed also to support other activities of the person, which he desires to conduct.

Equal access to goods instead of salaries

As it was noted above, the basic difference between capitalistic and holistic systems is that the last does not uses finances, goods and services as a form of reward and as a tool for social stratification of people, but as things which are due to them as exercising of legal rights. If a good is rare commodity and it cannot be provided to all participants, it does not go into the mass of offered goods, until conditions are not created that it can be distributed to all, who desire it.

In a holistic organization equal access to public goods means that every participant is free to use and not paying for a product in certain quantities, which is created with the resources of the organization and which is set for distribution.

We have to stress that the remuneration of the labor in capitalistic economy is not in real goods and services, but in currency. This means that people are dependent on the markets and good will of the merchants. Every currency can suffer devaluation and every product may increase its price at some point, so people live in constant struggle for survival.

7. Attitude of both systems towards material objects

The attitudes towards things, which are encouraged in a holistic society, are very different than those of capitalism.

In capitalistic states the main purpose of the material objects are to be:
- Central focus point of human existence;
- Means for satisfying needs;
- Means for coercing someone to do something;
- Indicator for social significance and influence;
- Means for making a profit;
- Means for creating dependencies among the participants;
- Means for maintaining social stratification among people

In the holistic society material objects are considered as:
- means for satisfying the needs of the participants;
- result from respectful interaction with Earth, animals and plants;
- means for maintaining the independence of the holistic community and of its participants from other subjects;
- means for application of the principle of equality among people;
- condition for achieving harmony. The provision of different products in sufficient quality and quantity is a requirement for the person to live freely, creatively, to be happy and to develop himself in a desired direction.
- means for inclusion of new participants;
- means for achieving of political and ideological influence over capitalistic organizations and their participants, who desire to trade with holistic organizations. When holistic communities become sufficiently resistant, the created products in addition to the needs of the participants would be needed only for external influence. Its direction should always be in service to the whole.

Limitations in usage of products and access to information

For the healthy functioning of every society it is necessary to exist certain limitations of access to information or the right to use specific type of products. An illustrating example is access to codes for nuclear weapons, which is granted to very limited number of officials in the state. All present day functioning limitations, related to age, professional qualification and personal rights, should be preserved in the holistic organization, after it makes a thorough research, whether they are in the interest of the whole. Such appropriate limitations are brought today in intellectual property creations, alcohol, right to drive a transport vehicle, etc.

The freedom of access to goods in the holistic community is not absolute, as it had never been in any other social form of organization. The difference is that in the holistic organization are determined limitations and access in the interest of the whole, after solid argumentation about why they are needed. In the egoistic systems access and limitations to information and goods are legally determined by a small group of people, who have selfish pursue of power and the interest of the whole is disregarded.

8. Limitations of the quantities of goods

To be included a product into the list of public property, which is set for distribution among the participants it has to be accessible for all, who desire it. Therefore, it is necessary these goods to be in quantities, which allow to be satisfied the demand among the people.

The determination of the limitations of quantities of public goods in the holistic organization should be done like every other activity - in regard to the interests of the subject of the holistic model and in satisfaction of the needs of the participants. Abundance is a desired state of the holistic system and it has to be achieved for every participant. Therefore, the limitations are conducted first of all to be applied the principle of equal access to goods. If a participant is willing to possess more goods or goods of higher quality, it is his right to trade with his own private property and to sell his labor as it is done in the capitalistic society.

As abundance is an aim for the holistic society, so overproduction, overconsumption and lack of needed goods and services are unwanted results for the holistic economy, because they are an evidence for poor management of the resources.

The holistic system exists to respond of the needs of all its participants. It takes into regard that different people have different preferences towards goods and services. For one person it can be desirable to consume larger quantities from a particular good and the holistic organization would adapt itself towards satisfying his needs, without regards that other people would not like to consume this particular good or like to have it in lower quantities.

Every participant will make individual choices of what he wants and in what quantities and the holistic organization would have the obligation to set the most appropriate quantitative limitations, so that a healthy balance is found between the interests of the participant, the community and the whole.

The criterion for distribution of public resources is not reduced to exactly the same quantities of goods for everyone, but to reaching the same level of satisfaction of the same need. For example a person, who weighs 100 kg would probably need more larger quantity of food, than someone, who weighs 60 kg. The equality of access to goods in this example is achieved with different quantities of food, which should be accessible for both participants. The scarcity of quality, healthy food is unthinkable for even one participant in a holistic organization, which cannot be valid for the capitalistic system.

The holistic society regulates its economy and labor process, guided by the desires of its participants. The created goods should be sufficient for everyone, in order people to feel relaxed and happy.

Another example for achieving equality in satisfying of the needs by different usage of resources is the building of a house for a person with disability, for a taller person, for a smaller person, for a participant with larger weight, etc.

The satisfaction, which brings the usage of a certain product, is also subjective. In capitalistic society there is class division on economic principle and if a product is considered as highly valued for a representative of one class, it may be disinteresting for representatives of a higher class. This type of differentiated attitude towards the same goods is dictated from different egoistic mentality and it is irrelevant for the building of a holistic society.

The system of service to the whole responds individually to the needs of every participant and it may use different quantity of resources in the search for equality of the level of satisfaction.

9. Access to goods and services from the same class

What is going to motivate people to work, if they receive goods and service with the same quality, without regards their type of position and profession?

The equal access to goods and services is a precondition for stimulating the driving force of service to the whole in the functioning of the holistic economy. All professions, which have been approved by the holistic organization, are necessary for the whole system and are bringing harmony for the participants and the whole.

Luxury goods, which at some point of development of the organization, cannot be replicated and produced in sufficient quantities for everyone, who desire them, should not be included in the scope of products for distribution. Definitely, they should not be used as a reward for high officials and managers of the organization, as it had been adopted in egoistic societies. The mentality that a person should please his own ego or the one of someone else, without being interested in the needs of the whole, is considered as deviant for the holistic system and the holistic organization aims to limit and not encourage it. This outlook, which place in the center of existence egoism, is unacceptable for the holistic society, because it leads to blinding for the problems of others, ignorance and suffering.

The absence of several basic labor functions in a society would lead to its fast decline and inability of having a working economy, than other labor positions. This does not mean that the first should be treated as more important than the second and therefore these employees should earn more than the others.

The holistic system aims to organize itself in a way to stimulate the participants to choose a profession, which is their desired form of self-expression and service to the whole, and not just a means for existence, enrichment and gaining of capital.

Through the application of the principal of equal access to goods and services, created with public resources, the people would much easily focus their attention on what they want to create and to do and in what direction they want to develop society. Labor becomes the needed form of creation and project participation. The difference in remuneration in capitalistic society in many cases causes confusion among people, because the social status of a profession or the higher payment mutes the inner voice of personal realization. Instead of following this voice, people often choose more convenient and economically stable path of professional development, which does not always bring them satisfaction, joy and spiritual development.

The role of the holistic organization is to create conditions for the person to receive knowledge and skill to perform his labor and encourages this direction of development, which suits the interests of the whole in the best possible way. Therefore, access to goods and services is irrelevant for the choice of profession.

The high quality of the work of every employee is important for the proper functioning of the holistic economy and for the provision of quality products and services to the participants. In egoistical economic systems the approach for stimulating quality work performance is in the form of financial and non-pecuniary rewards, where as poor performance is avoided by enforcing sanctions. Priority for a working person in egoistical organization is how much he receives in the end of the day and not what he produces with his efforts and talents. This is the reason why in egoistic systems there is replacement of values, unlawful benefits, corruption and career development without knowledge and experience. These phenomena are always happening in egoistic societies and then the rewards are often not received by the people, who follow the rules and are the best performers, but by those, who are capable to exploit the system for personal gain. One of the biggest systematic problems of the egoistic systems is that political power and managing positions are considered to be a prize, because they guarantee more stable surviving of the person, who possesses them in detriment of the governed. This is the reason of the unstoppable conflict between the ruling elite and the governed, which results in power play manipulations, oppression, exploitation and hiding of needed information and other resources in order to maintain control over weak people.

In many occasions the egoistic states develop upon the citizens the mentality that certain official should receive additional benefits just for performing his official duties. When this attitude is present, such an official does not understand the true purpose of his profession and he is not taking responsibility of his actions, because he is serving his ego.

The result is erosion of the whole system, loss confidence in the state and gradual decline of the social relations. Such an employee could never find solutions for the challenges of the society.

Societies, which are based on egoistic economic and political systems, are doomed to be governed poorly, because the governance is in the interest of the ruling party and not in the interests of the community or even less - to the whole. Financial, banking and insurance sectors and big corporations count on limitation of access to goods and services for the people, in order to profit from their labor to gain them. Therefore, the abundance and economic freedom would never become a reality for most of the people in egoistic societies. They are severing the natural bonds with nature and with other subjects only to see their inevitable socio-political implosion. The loss of trust in the system is undesired result for the ruling elite and that is why they are going to "invest" in poor education, weak information capabilities of citizens, so that most of the people are unable to understand in depth the internal conflicts and problems that the system is creating.

Holistic governance does not use methods for increasing of the ego as a form of reward and its decreasing as a sanction. Holistic methods of stimulation of quality work performance are used instead. Such methods are clarification of the responsibility that a person has to society in general and towards a concrete community in particular. Labor is presented as an opportunity to fulfill this responsibility. The awareness of the employees is raised also with knowledge about their potential development as people, if they choose to follow one professional path or another. Another motivation for quality of work performance is the opening of the access to career development and having more responsibilities, if the person is capable to handle them. The quality of the work is the relevant criteria for career development.

If an employee does not want to do his job with care and with high quality, the impact of his poor performance would be narrowed, but not his access to goods and services. The holistic organization should look for the reasons why this person is not willing to participate fully in the organization and with them the positive forms of motivation. If criminal behavior is present, holistic methods should be applied together with the institute of humane restorative reaction, which is described in chapter seven.

10. Motivation of the employee

The holistic management of labor foresees that the work should be useful for the whole and also should develop the person, who is conducting it. Both aspects are not regarded in capitalistic system and presently there are many professions, which are not developing significantly the people, who are having them. Whether a labor is beneficial for the person is secondary and sometimes completely disregarded factor by the private employer, who is designing the job characteristics. Modern capitalistic economy is driven by the selfish interests of states and corporations, whereas holistic economy is functioning in the interests of the whole. For this reason in capitalistic society is considered to be acceptable to preserve professions, which are harmful for the health of the person in all sectors of economy, such as coal mining. Despite that there are alternative means for gaining energy, despite that machines can be used in fields which are dangerous for the person the characteristics of the job remain unchanged.

From the viewpoint of humankind every profession should possess optimal low level of risk for the health of the person. In order certain labor to be useful for the employee it is necessary that it is chosen by the person not because of fear for survival, but because of the desire of contribution and positive impact in society. Motivation for conducting specific work is one of the main differences between both systems.

What do we really want to work, if we silence the egoistic motivation for money-making and for achieving social status and prestige?

How many hours per day do we want to work and how do we want to spend the rest of the time?

With our choice of profession and activities are we going to develop our personality in the areas, which our inner self is craving for?

What is the desired rhythm of life and do we feel supported enough by the system to create fulfilling relations with others?

Are we going to deepen our knowledge in areas, for which otherwise we do not have enough time?

Are we going to have more fun?

Ultimately, are we going to be happier?

One of the most important characteristics of every profession in a holistic organization is that the person, who is performing it should feel himself satisfied and truly willing to have it. The profession should be designed in a way that it becomes his tool for expression to bring harmony for the community. If this attitude is encouraged in society, it would be changed the way job descriptions are created. People would have much more opportunities to achieve their goals and dreams for professional realization, instead of being coerced to choose unsatisfactory job positions, so that they could put food on the table for their family and to maintain higher standard of living.

If a child shares to us that it desires to become a scientist, who is developing chemical weapons for mass destruction, or a military pilot, who wishes to drop an atomic bomb among peaceful citizens, or manufacturer of food, which is harmful to people's health, we are going to see that this child needs psychological or psychiatric support, if it has such dreams. However, when these professions actually exist, we do not demand from states and big corporation to apply common sense, be reasonable and having humane attitude. We miss to think what is right, because we are persuaded what is necessary for the survival of the people, or for some other stated reason. From a holistic point of view, it is neither necessary, neither it should be justified. People, who are exercising these and similar professions, most probably are doing these activities, because they are counting on the salary and because they are following orders of their superiors. These excuses do not decrease the burden that they are creating for themselves and for humankind.

The consequences from an action are not changed by the fact that they are socially acceptable and allowed. The appraisal of the society of a particular action may only signify the level of social development, but not the real effect from the deeds.

Economic relations in service to self unjustly deprive most of the people from access to goods and services. The products that they receive have not been created to be useful, pleasant and healthy for them, but to entice them to consume more. The employees do not receive direct access to goods and services, but money in specific currency. When the financial and economic system of a state collapse, affected are mostly the lower social classes. They are those, who lose their means for sustenance and the chance to provide decent living conditions for them and their families. Such financial cataclysms may be caused by people, or not, such as natural disasters. Severe negative economic results are caused also by financial speculations, competition for market territories, political sanctions. These economic downfalls are often perceived as legal and morally acceptable. They are justified by the states, even though that they lead to loss of human lives, poverty and inhumane development of social relations.

In the process of building of economic system in service to the whole, the focus would be not in artificial creation of low-skilled jobs, which are not providing vital service, or which can easily be replaced by machines. Instead, in holistic organizations should be created job positions, which are developing social and cognitive skills, emotional maturity, humane treatment and which are in service to the whole. The building of an economic system, which satisfies equally the needs of all participants in an optimal way, would be possible not from a perspective of achieving a balance between quality and price, but to achieve balance between quality and quantity. This means that in a holistic organization are created goods and services with optimal good quality, so that are satisfied the needs of all participants, who desire them. In application of this ratio, it is avoided reaching lavish luxury for a few and instead are produced high-quality goods and services for every participant.

For example, if we accept that the creation of a product with a golden covering is an extravagant luxury, for which it would hard and unjustified to be produced on mass level for everyone, then items with such covering would not be created with public resources. If for a person it is an insatiable whim, he is free to provide it, using the instruments and methods of capitalism and trade his labor and property, privately hire people to create his desired product with gold covering. Accordingly, the person is not restrained to satisfy his desires, but public resources of the holistic organization shall not be used for that purpose. Holistic society prioritizes the social challenges and the needs of people and it organizes itself to satisfy the corresponding class of needs for all people.

For the ratio "quality-price" the deciding factor is the market and the willingness of a corporation, or a state to provide a product. This often leads to shortages for people in need, or to the creation of low-quality products, because it is cheaper for a corporation.

For the ratio "quality-quantity" however, deciding factor is the needs of all participants in the holistic organization and the available resources to be used for their best satisfaction. The production and distribution of goods is following the principle of optimal quality for everyone, who desires the product.

The resources and energy, spared for marketing and commercials, which are influencing the needs of the people to buy harmful products, are going to be invested in improving the quality and the logistics with useful goods and service.

The next advantage of creating of socio-economic system, which satisfies the needs of all people, is the possibility of strategic long-term global planning with the best available technologies and experts. The result will be the provision of package of services, which is unprecedented in matter of quality, quantity and scope.

The participation in the labor process of all adults in the holistic organization is another huge advantage of the holistic organization. The absence of unemployment, the opportunities for a desired and meaningful job, which is developing the individual and takes up to six hours from his working day, would result to shift of social relations, inspiration, motivation for service to the whole and humanization of the economy.

CHAPTER 7

HUMANE RESTORATIVE REACTION

Every state creates its own legal norms, which determine the boundaries of exercised freedom of the people under its jurisdiction, so that the rights of others are not negatively affected. The holistic state is going to share the same principle. When violation of these norms happens, the states react towards the legal offender in the same way from thousands of years, using similar methods for sanctions. From Ancient times until present day law invariably bonds the due behavior with the sanction.

As main structural element of the legal norm, sanction is endued with function of social regulation. This means that modern law relies on guiding people's behavior with the threat of negative consequences in case of legal infringement.

The effectiveness of sanction presupposes that it is an undesired result for the person, who will suffer it. Legal regulation continues to rely on threatening and fear based norms which are supposed to regulate the behavior of people in all areas of social life.

Justice is still understood as imposition of symmetrical punishment for corresponding crime, and not as work on restoration of harmony of violated social relations.

The message which is contained in every legal norm and the way in which it reaches to the people represents the attitude of the egoistic state towards its citizens.

Sanctions are always directed towards the ego of the person, in order to regulate his behavior. It can be in different forms: from a speeding ticket to imprisonment and even death penalty for the perpetrator of unlawful deeds. In the legal norms of egoistic systems is intrinsic the approach of threatening of the person's ego, if he violates the prescribed behavior. Such legal formula foresees indirect bans for specific actions, which are considered by the legislator as negative, instead of positive encouragement of harmonious social relations. Let's take for example a norm, which has its equivalent in the criminal law of all states: "This, who deliberately kills another, shall be punished for homicide by imprisonment from 10 to 20 years".[34] It does not invite us to honor the life of our fellow, to live in spirit of mutual understanding and with the attitude to resolve peacefully the challenges that we face between each other. Instead of positive direction, the legal norm is structured on thousands of years old formula of explaining what would happen to a person, who kills another one.

Logically arises the question whether people are truly not killing each other, because of fear of jail? Do we want this to be their guiding motivation of not doing homicides, instead of honoring human life? This method of "prevention" of crimes did not lead to reduction or elimination of crimes as a whole and the homicides in particular in all countries until present day and it will not lead in the future!

The humane approach towards all individuals is a trustworthy sign for positive development of a civilization and a tendency in modern societies which should be irreversible, including to those representatives of society, who behave extremely inhumane. Natural result of this approach is the abatement of the repressive elements of sanctions, particularly the punishment of imprisonment in criminal law.

Important indicator of the dying social role of the punishment of imprisonment as a basic method of social regulation is the religious terrorism. Obviously there is no legal sanction, which could act deterrent for those, who are motivated to conduct suicidal terrorist acts to receive their status recognition as a "reward in Heaven". In most of the criminal acts, the perpetrators are fully aware of the sanctions for their deeds, but they are able to overcome the fear and are ready to accept the consequences, on the condition that they are captured and properly convicted.

In the systems of service to the whole the violation of legal norms is perceived as an occurring of knot in social relations. The cutting of the knot should be the last means of action after all other attempts for resolving the conflict are made. Considerable initial efforts should be made to unravel the particular knot and to search for the deeper reasons for its occurring. Therefore, in those more developed societies are not going to be repressive sanctions, which we are seeing today, but instead, will be used methods, which we can call humane restorative. Instead of a sanction, which corresponds to a committed violation of a norm, the organ, which is responsible for the social relations in the service to the

---

34 Art.115 of *Criminal Code of Republic of Bulgaria*, in force in 1968

whole, is going to use the legal institute of the **humane restorative reaction**. Essentially it is an alternative of all types of legal sanctions and its purpose, as it is seen from its name, is to restore the humanity in an individual and the harmony of social relations. This institute is not created to cause fear to the potential perpetrator of criminal act; it does not reduce his property status; it does not restrict his other rights, which is conducted by the punishments in criminal law. The establishing of this new legal institute is going to create an environment for recovery and restoration of the humane and good inside the person.

The organs, which are going to implement this new institute, have to be able to look upon every human being as a manifestation of the Absolute and to look for the spark of living light, from which the person may have strayed far away and may even don't know that it exist in him. This primordial knowledge and personal perception are going to provide a chance for the person, who has committed a crime to find his higher self, his true purpose and ways of being in harmony with himself and with society.

From psychological point of view everyone, who had violated legal norms, should be supported and encouraged to become conscious about his act, to take responsibility for it, to distinguish himself from the criminal attitude and if it is possible to take actions for fixing the damages. Precisely these stages should be applied in humane restorative reaction and in this exact sequence. The institute includes limitation of the freedom of moving of the person similarly to the punishment of imprisonment with the aim of preventing him to commit another criminal act. The difference is that the first is conducted as a form of therapeutic seclusion with intensive psychological work with the person and the second resembles throwing away in a dungeon. The purpose of limitation of the freedom of moving is not to threaten him, but to work together with the person on becoming conscious about the different aspects of the harmful results of his actions. In order to achieve that level of self-awareness, it is necessary to overcome the internal criminal attitude, which had led to the criminal act. The aim of the humane restorative reaction is to support the perpetrator to become aware about the misbalance of his values and attitudes, which is leading to unlawful behavior. This type of work with the person resembles medical intervention, which aims to recover the patient and similarly to it the sick should be temporarily limited, as long as continues his treatment. Similarly to the medical intervention, humane restorative reaction should be conducted by professionally trained specialists; it should be diagnosed and individualized for the particular person; conducted safely, painlessly and with care. Another important aspect is that the person, who is subjected to it, should be willing to undergo these actions. Many people would accredit this attitude to the modern punishment, but this is not true at all. It is enough to mention that most of the criminal acts are recidivistic, which means that the sanction did not manage to reeducate the people and they have committed other criminal acts. If the punishment was dedicated to be beneficial for the character of the perpetrator, it would not be necessary for him to have an attorney, who de facto is trying to avoid the sanctions. Instead the perpetrator would have hired a person, who is going to encourage him to confess and put himself under the "rehabilitation effect" of the punishment. If punishment had such a positive effect, many people alone would have search for it, even before the perpetration of criminal acts. All these are not a fact and we should distinguish the roles of humane restorative reaction and the punishment of imprisonment.

Humane restorative reaction, contrary to the imprisonment, is not disregarding other rights of the perpetrator, which are essential for his rehabilitation and harmonization of his values. For example, the punishment of imprisonment is a sanction, which separate the person from the environment of his family and places him among other convicted people. This act alone maintains his personal identification as a criminal. We are not going to be wrong, if we conclude that cases of soaring of the personality and harmonization of the behavior are very rare in the prisons of all states. Modern prison is not designed and managed like a university, like a monetary, or like a hospital, where a person can be released from his aggression, disrespect of other people's rights and criminal attitudes. Humane restorative reaction also separates the person from society in the interests of both. The term for this separation is in time frame, which is needed for the person to overcome his criminal attitudes. In this period he should receive adequate psychological support for his problem, which has to lead to improvement of his character and recovery of his humane attitude. The measures for separation and follow-up work with the person should be conducted with respect to his rights and encouraging those relationships, which could be beneficial for his recovery and are his resource for improvement. For example such relationships might be his family and relatives, who are having positive influence over the person. This means that meetings and communication with these people would be facilitated by the expert group, which is responsible for the person, and they would be much more regular than the visitations in a modern prison. Meetings with the family partner and the children should be facilitated every day, if their bond is having positive effect in the process of rehabilitation.

Modern day punishment of imprisonment consists of three fundamental internal incongruities, which are not in service to the whole:

- It is simultaneously supposed to cause fear preventively and has the task to correct the person, when it is imposed. If after enduring a punishment the person is ethically harmonized and purified by his tormenting criminal attitudes, then it should not cause fear among people and it should have been strongly encouraged by the state and by attorneys. People would have desired punishments, if they have such positive effects, that the criminal law foresees for them.

- The second internal conflict is visible in the notion that if we put together many perpetrators of criminal acts in one place, they would become better people, maybe following the mathematical rule that multiplying negatives becomes a plus. The analysis shows that the relations in prisons are creating new durable criminal attitudes and strong bonds between the prisoners. Many prisoners also become victims of crimes inside the facilities, but such acts are tolerated by society and institutions, because violation of their human rights is seen as a form of justice.

- The third internal incongruity is related with the deprivation of the prisoners of regular contact with those people and with those activities, which could be beneficial for their character building and positive for their ethical harmonization. Without professional work in this direction, it is very hard the redemption to occur. Instead the convicted to receive different forms of education, reeducation and positive social bonds, he is offered...a criminal environment.

Distinctive feature of the humane restorative reaction is that it can be applied in the modern penitentiary systems of states, if their representatives have the wisdom and will to do it. When holistic organizations are institutionalized, this institute should become the permanent substitutions of punishment of imprisonment.

Humane restorative reaction is composed of four basic stages of influence to the perpetrator of criminal acts and they are the following:

I. Separation from society
II. Therapeutic impact
III. Restoration
IV. Integration back to society

I. The first stage of separation of the person from society is overlapping to a large extent with the punishment of imprisonment in modern penitentiary systems. However, there is one crucial difference between both and it is that humane restorative reaction may be provided as a service to a person, who desires to receive psychological support or physical protection from the holistic state. People are going to be aware that in all stages and all methods that are going to be used will be in their interest and without harming them. Such separation may be provided even if the person has not committed criminal act, if he desires to harmonize his ethics, emotions and actions, before violation of legal norms.

This stage is needed both for the person and for the society, which is (could be) harmed by criminal activities. As was stated above the separation can be compulsory or voluntary. It should be stated clearly that compulsory separation is prohibited for a person, who is not sentenced for committing a crime. Separation from society should be conducted on a place, where the person is not going to be in an unsupervised contact with other people, who have committed crimes. It is absolutely necessary the person initially to meet with the team of therapists, who are going to work with him and only with those relatives and close persons, who are going to make a positive impact on him. From the moment of starting therapeutic work with the person to become aware about the consequences of his own actions and taking responsibility for them, is when the humane restorative reaction moves into its second stage - therapeutic impact.

II. The purpose of this stage is the person to become aware of his actions, taking responsibility for them and providing the opportunity for the person to distance himself from his criminal attitudes. In order to achieve these objectives, a team of experts should be formed for every case. They have to build individual strategy for work with the person. Key distinction with modern methods of work with convicted people is the role of guilt.

Guilt is the state of being responsible for the commission of an offense. In relation to humane restorative reaction it is undesired psychological state, because the person is identifying his whole personality with his criminal activity and he is blaming himself, instead of building his character and ethics. Therapeutic work and catharsis is largely hindered by the feeling of guilt. In humane restorative reaction guilt is replaced by gradual transition of four psychological states:

1. Becoming conscious of the actions and their consequences;
2. Taking responsibility for them;
3. Looking for the psychological reasons, which have led to the criminal attitudes and behavior;
4. Intention for change and personal harmonization.

The team of experts is supposed to be formed in such a way, so that in includes psychological therapy, social interventions and all other forms of influence, which could direct the person or facilitate his efforts for life in service to the whole. It is necessary to form unique team of such experts for every person, who is submitted to humane restorative reaction. All activities, used methods and techniques should be documented in order to develop the program with knowledge of good practices.

III. When the person has cultivated the intention for personal harmonization, starts the stage of restoration of his natural humanity. It can occur only on his will and pressure should not be placed upon him. If such will is absent and the person is not truly intending to change his attitudes and behavior, the work stops on the previous stage.

The purpose of the third stage is to be facilitated the intention of the person for change, by providing him the opportunity to compensate his criminal acts in the best possible way. In order to be effective the work of the team of experts, they should carefully prepare and individual rehabilitation program. It should consist of such activities, which are going to establish harmonious pattern of behavior and higher ethical code for the individual.

IV. When the term of the sentence expires, the person should choose whether to return to society or not. The task of the team is to prepare him and partially the society for his successful integration. The personal decision is what distinguishes the humane restorative reaction from the punishment of imprisonment. At this stage of final transition, the team of experts should include the relatives and close people to the person. This delicate preparation should include multiple aspects and its positive effects are important for both the person and the society.

All modern criminal and penitentiary legal systems are proclaiming similar objectives, which they desire to reach through punishment:

1) The convicted to be corrected and taught to observe the law;

2) To alert him and to deny the opportunity to commit another criminal act;

3) To apply correctional influence and to warn other members of society.[35]

What does the humane restorative reaction contribute more than the punishment of imprisonment to achieve these objectives?

1. The separation from society in the first does not aim to deprive the person of his other rights, which are protected by the law. On the contrary, the convicted should be able to exercise them, as long as it does not interfere with his therapeutic work. The team, which is conducting the processes of therapy and reintegration, shall allow more frequent contacts with people, who are having positive influence on the person.

2. Humane restorative reaction may be applied on person, who is not sentenced, but who is willing to receive adequate psychological support before committing a crime. This makes the new legal institute much more effective in relation to prevention.

---

35 Art. 36, par.1. of *Criminal Code of Republic of Bulgaria*, in force in 1968

3. The convicted should not be placed from the beginning among other people, who have committed a crime and who would have negative influence in the process of his correction of character. For every convicted person should be dedicated a place, where he could be in contact with the team of experts and with the people appointed for his case.

4. The process of correction of his behavior and of intensive psychological work with him, before he is released is going to guarantee much better that he is not going to commit such criminal acts. After the expiration date and the finishing of the work with the person, he has to choose to return back to society, in order to bear responsibility for his actions. This principle is also important with the fact that it facilitates the opportunity for the convicted to forgive himself and to find the strength to contribute positively to the society.

5. Another important feature of the humane restorative reaction is that the person is going to be much more prepared and supported to be fully integrated in society and not thrown back in it. The last is typical for the penal systems and it is an irresponsible act to society and to the person.

Humane restorative reaction does not use violence, threat, torture and unproductive deprivation of rights to the person, who have committed a crime. Therefore, the new institute is not in contradiction with any of the legal systems in the world. Despite the fact that it is not presently implemented, there are not legal boundaries this institute to be introduced in the legislation of separate states, which are not holistic yet. It is a natural result of intensifying the humane approach towards every person and it applies values, which are declared by most nations.

The introduction of the humane restorative reaction as a better alternative of the punishment of imprisonment is going to result in positive transformation of the roles of all actors in the litigation process:

1. The motivation of the accused to avoid the punishment is going to be substituted with one to cooperate for the disclosure of all needed facts in relation to the crime. If the person had committed a crime, the state is going to provide him with psychological support, therapy and character development program in a separated and managed environment.

2. The interests and main functions of judges, prosecution, legal counsel and team of experts are focused on harmonization of the values of the perpetrator and his rehabilitation. In this way the court trial would resemble a council for appointment of therapy for the person, which is looking for the causes of the criminal acts. Combining the limitation of free movement with intensive psychological work shall turn the reaction of the state into means, which is useful for the perpetrator, but also for society. This undoubtedly would lead to more cases of cooperation of the accused to disclose the truth around the criminal action than we are seeing today.

3. Even if we have the perfect methods for disclosure of truth, in relation to psychological work with the convicted it is important that he makes the first step to confess and to support the authorities in understanding the facts. The convicted is stimulated to cooperate with them, because they have to act in his best interest alongside with the best interest of society.

The holistic overview of the contemporary litigation reveals that there is interrelation between all participants in the process. Theoretically, if all state officials are performing brilliantly their tasks, the perpetrator is still not going to be positively transformed and the crime rate would remain the same, because criminal attitudes are not treated in advance and afterwards. Therefore, we should fairly admit that the modern litigation is unable to reach the goals for reduction of crimes and elevating the ethics of the perpetrators of criminal acts.

4. After judicial establishing of the facts around a criminal act, the main focus of the humane restorative reaction would not be to choose how many years the person should be separated from society. The primary goal is going to be determination of a program for correctional behavior with a team of experts for a term which would be sufficient.

5. The creation of an overall mechanism for implementation of the humane restorative reaction would be a humane act to the perpetrator, but also to society, which is an environment that allowed, stimulated, or ignored the formation of criminal attitudes. This institute would contribute to the real reduction

of crimes. Every crime is a choice of a person to violate social values, but also a result, which shows that the society is unable to involve the person to these values. Through humane restorative reaction responsibility are going to take both the perpetrator and whole society, which had let the lower attitudes and the formation of criminal patterns of behavior. An opportunity would be presented for a person and a society to heal the wounds together. Society also requires thorough care and therapeutic treatment, when a crime is committed, because one of his members had decided to violate deeply its values. Main objective of the humane restorative reaction is to investigate deeply the reasons for occurring of the crime and for the violation of social values. Such analysis is needed to improve the mechanisms for integration of people and social relations in order to prevent criminal activity. For example, if the crime is committed of anger, the guiding focus of social work should be upon anger therapy, emotional maturity and cultivating mutual respect among people. If the crime is theft, the focus should be on the role of goods in society, cultivation of respect towards the rights of private property, inviolability of people and legal ways of acquisition of desired goods. Every person is perceived as microcosms, which is a manifestation of the whole and representation of humankind. Therefore, his unique worldview is needed and important for society.

6. Humane restorative reaction is not an effeminate or naïve method of social intervention to a perpetrator in which the victim is ignored. It is an opportunity which society provides for the person to develop his ethics and behavior and then to be accepted back in society.

Let asks ourselves: is society protected, when a convicted person is released from a prison with a criminal environment? In many cases such a person is even more dangerous for the community, because he had cultivated in the prison even twisted attitudes. The correctional and therapeutic work with the person is the means, which may satisfy the interest of the person, of humankind, of society and of the whole.

The holistic approach of work with the perpetrator of criminal acts includes thorough analysis of the weaknesses of social relations, which had led to such violation of norms. Society can be deeply understood precisely by using this approach. When the humane restorative reaction is implemented in a holistic state, there would be an important feature, which does not exist in a state with a repressive penitentiary system. In a holistic state the person had declared that he will live by the main principles of holistic society and that he will follow the legal norms, whereas in modern states the rule of law is imposed over people. This significant difference predetermines the approach for intervention. When there is agreement and coherence of the wills of a person and society, the correction is aimed at overcoming the inability of the person to keep his commitment to the norms in service to the whole.

CONCLUSION

The ideal for holistic society is higher than those for national or religious domination of one civilization or an alliance of states. It stands above the idea of united humankind, which is going to be egoistic towards other living beings, including Earth. The strength of holistic society is not in the present in the skill to use several of its members to subjugate the others, but it is in the ability to develop a harmonious environment to all, who are willing to live with regards to the interests of to the whole.

The holistic organizations will be able to develop themselves steadily, if they succeed to create and implement policies, which are satisfying the interests of the whole.

The establishing of solid holistic organizations in different states by participants, who share the principles of holistic society, may become into the living light of Earth and other places, where humanism and respect of life is going to be protected.

Holistic society mounts the spiritual bond between humankind and Earth, as well as the responsibility of humans towards all living beings on the planet.

The holistic organizations should be able to become islands of peace and harmony, which are capable to protect themselves from all external and internal encroachments. They have to be able to achieve these tasks without violating the principles of respect towards other subjects and in regard to their sovereign rights to choose their path of existence. Global planning and management of all processes in a way which satisfies the interests of the whole will release this powerful driving force of society much more than we are seeing it presently. The principle of economic self-sufficiency, provision of public goods and services as a form of right and not as a reward, the absence of internal struggle for survival, and the careful choice of external partners will make the holistic organizations capable and strong subjects. The vision of life, based on spiritual self-awareness and on relations of regarding the interests of all living beings is the cornerstone around which shall be established the legal system, the political life and the economy. The comprehension and the feeling of unity between all will lead to new holistic vision of governance in which selfishness will step aside its dominant role to the driving force of service to the whole.

Aleksandar Milanov

HOLISTIC SOCIETY

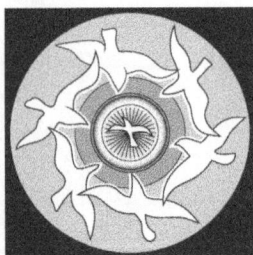

Author: © Aleksandar Slavkov Milanov, 2017
You may support the vision of holistic society by making a donation on our website: www.newagecitizens.org
The e-mail of the author is: alexander.milanov.nac@gmail.com
ISBN 978-619-90834-2-0